A PRACTICAL GUIDE FOR TEACHERS OF ADULT LEARNERS

By Mary Hale Barry and Daniel Byram

A PRACTICAL GUIDE FOR TEACHERS OF ADULT LEARNERS

Publisher: Channel Custom Publishing, San Diego, CA

Manufactured in the United States of America, 1st edition, Curriculum Technology, LLC, 2020.

A PRACTICAL GUIDE FOR TEACHERS OF ADULT LEARNERS, 1st Edition. A textbook by Curriculum Technology, LLC. San Diego, California. 1st edition, 2021.

ISBN SBN-10: ISBN-13: 978-1-938087-40-0

TABLE OF CONTENTS

ABOUT THE AUTHORS

MARY BARRY

Mary Barry is a Postsecondary Education Executive, with experience in multiple key campus positions and as Chief Academic Officer for several career education industry leaders. With instructor experience in the adult classroom and as the Director of Academic Affairs for the Southern California campus of the University of Phoenix (UOP), she worked with faculty leaders to develop a highly effective program for onboarding new faculty which became the model for all of UOP to prepare thousands of working professionals to teach in the adult classroom.

Upon leaving UOP and transitioning to the C-Suite in 1998, her responsibilities included New Program Development, Institutional and Programmatic Accreditation, Faculty and Student Services, Academic Quality Assurance, and Internal Audit. Mary served two national accreditors as an elected Commissioner and as a member of Standards Review and Preliminary Review committees. She was a visiting team member for various accreditors in their mission to evaluate institutional readiness for initial and renewed grants of accreditation. In the past five years, Mary was the Chief Strategy Officer for Curriculum Technology LLC, and the Private Sector Advisor for Elsevier Education. Previous to her work in career education management, Mary was a banking executive and served as Public Affairs Officer in the U.S. Marine Corps.

She earned a bachelor's degree in Secondary Education from Bowling Green State University, an MBA from Northwestern University, and a Juris Doctorate from Thomas Jefferson School of Law.

DAN BYRAM

Dan Byram is a veteran law enforcement executive, an educator in both private and public post-secondary sectors, author, and business owner. Dan is a retired police lieutenant from Mesa, Arizona, having served as Academy Director and with extensive experience in Intelligence, both Covert and Tactical Operations, and Training. Dan taught in the Community College system of Arizona for over 15 years prior to assuming administrative and leadership responsibilities for a dozen years in private sector education. There he served as Department Chair, Campus Director of Education and as Academic Program Director responsible for development, support and outcomes monitoring of Criminal Justice training programs.

Leveraging his experience in law enforcement and education, in 2005 Dan founded Curriculum Technology LLC, a full-service curriculum development business which incorporates program planning and design, technology integration, publication of textbooks and learning materials, and hosting and delivery services in online and blended learning environments.

Dan holds a Bachelor of Arts in Management from the University of Phoenix and a Master of Arts Degree in Human Behavior from Remington College. Dan is a member of the Phi Theta Kappa International Honor Society for Community Colleges and holds a lifetime teaching certificate from Arizona Community Colleges.

INTRODUCTION

Welcome to the Career College classroom! You are embarking on an exciting journey that will challenge you in many ways, and the rewards will be innumerable.

Teachers find their way to the career college classroom in various ways. All are subject matter experts in a professional field such as medical, business, law enforcement, information technology, and construction trades. All are formally educated in their professional area, but typically not in the education sciences. For career schools, attracting experienced working professionals to the classroom is critical for training students in just the right hands-on and soft skills that employers are looking for.

In a career school, the instructor's professional work experience trumps teaching experience. If you lack professional working experience, students will not get what they signed up for. You have both technical and soft skills in your teaching area that were gained through your professional life. With that, you can learn how to teach! Teaching skills – both the technical and interpersonal skills required – can be taught and will develop and improve over time with commitment and practice.

YOU are just what a career school is looking for.

This book will not "train" you how to teach in ten easy lessons. Our purpose is to provide working professionals - new to the classroom - with critical knowledge about career schools, the students they serve, how adult students learn, and the classroom management issues you are sure to encounter. Even if you are an experienced educator, you may not have had access to this contextual information. We hope you will find value here too.

Your teaching skills will develop over time. All the material, examples, and suggestions here reflect our collective personal experience. Our expertise was not developed overnight and, like most things, often came from first not knowing or making mistakes. And we are still learning.

We hope this book will help you, whether you are a new or experienced instructor, to develop and continuously improve your teaching.

"A teacher development program in a box, designed by and for career college educators, with career college students in mind. Imminently practical. "

Buck Garrett, J.D.
Partner, Champion Education, Hunan, China; Veteran Educator and Community Service Volunteer

PREFACE

Teachers play a critical role in our lives – Seventy percent of us recall at least one teacher who had an exceptionally positive impact on our life. What a privilege to know that we change lives through our life's work!

I always liked school. I even played school at home with my siblings when I was very young. And for as long as I remember I wanted to be a teacher. For women of my generation, teaching was one of only a handful of viable female occupations. I was fine with that.

Still, like many others, I had my share of unpleasant experiences with teachers and the learning process. One day in second grade, Sister Mary Margaret denied me permission to use the restroom; and when I had an accident. I was mercilessly teased by all the other kids for weeks. Often during elementary school, I would bring home a straight-A report card; but, ironically, always with multiple check marks for talking too much or not being able to stay in my seat all day. I fought back tears more than once when I wasn't picked to clean the chalkboard erasers at the end of the school day. A chaotic home life seriously impacted my senior year high school grades, but I would never have considered asking a teacher for extra time or other accommodations. I suffered quietly and with a few bad grades. No one noticed. In my third year of college, I received an "F" on an assignment for a children's book analysis that was "so good it must have been plagiarized." This resulted in a "D" for the course; I did not know how to fight back. Of all the world class professors in my MBA program, I don't recall any one of them that knew our names, our career focus, or our management concerns. Upon graduating law school, I failed one section of the bar exam on my first take because I was pregnant, debilitated with morning sickness, and couldn't sufficiently focus on the massive preparation for all the tests. These experiences, and others, made me feel isolated and unworthy. Despite the fact that I also enjoyed many positive school experiences over the years, and was considered a very good student, I still feel a tinge of embarrassment and hurt these many years later for the slights and failures.

The classroom can be the avenue to career and personal success; and yet is fraught with fear, disappointment, and failure for too many students. In fact, more than half of all students who start college end up dropping out before graduation. What a waste of potential!

Most students' negative experiences are far worse than any of mine. Sadly, negative experiences in the classroom can have lasting effects, significantly impeding a person's personal development as well as their professional advancement. As teachers, we must be ever mindful of our impact on the students we serve. Everybody is going through something. People are sensitive. We all take things personally. And so, we not only have to know our stuff, but we also have to understand how our knowledge and expertise is successfully imparted to our students. This requires not only vast knowledge of our teaching area (you've got that) but the continuing demonstration of an effective array of interpersonal skills that sets an encouraging and supportive tone in all student interactions.

I've been fortunate to practice my teaching profession in public, private and for-profit institutions as a reading tutor, as both an elementary and high school teacher, as a trainer and as a university professor. Eventually I found my home in adult career education. It's here you will find students who are not necessarily academically well-groomed, but who have a vision of significantly improving their lives through education. And it's here I found that as a teacher you will encounter no greater need to exercise self-awareness, compassion, and integrity.

Every school I attended from kindergarten through college provided for teaching and learning in a traditional teacher-centric model. This model assumes the teacher is the expert. It embodies a didactic approach to the subject where lectures from the podium and note taking are pretty much it. Traditional teaching and learning methods focus primarily on rote learning (reading, lecture, and memorization) and testing through recitation of facts. Often, if you have the facts right, regardless of your understanding or ability to apply them in real life, you'll get good grades. Having learned and practiced other teaching-learning models since my early days, I see the traditional model in its extreme as a "take it or leave it" proposition with students as winners or losers. Sure, some students will excel in this model; but most adult students in particular don't like it and don't thrive in it. For them, something is missing. Career schools serve these students!

Through all of my classroom experience, I learned that successful teaching and student learning do not occur naturally, or by happenstance. Even after studying education science and practicing as a student teacher, I really wasn't a particularly good teacher at 22 years old. I had the science and theory down but was deficient in experience of course. It took a while to learn how to connect with students, to know how deep and wide a lesson should be for a given period of time, and how to accurately evaluate performance and assign grades. Excellent teaching encompasses knowledge of your teaching area, learning science, the psychology of instructor-student relationships and the willingness to keep getting better at the craft.

To be sure, positive teacher-student interactions will have an equally lasting impact on your students. And by positive, I don't mean socialize with students, tell jokes, be an easy grader, or lower the standards. Teachers who impress students are straight shooters, treat all students with respect, apply the rules evenhandedly and teach their hearts out to get lessons through to students! I still remember the difference a teacher's reassuring word made, or how a teacher persisted in teaching a difficult point until we all got it, or when a professor took the time to add an encouraging comment on a paper. There's nothing as inspiring as an instructor seeing something positive in you, especially when you don't even know you have it. I've had all of these experiences throughout the years and carry them and the teachers who gifted them to me in my heart to this day.

All the best in your new adventure, and may you have an exceptionally positive impact on many students' lives!

Mary Barry

My journey into private post-secondary education took an unusual path. I began teaching as a police academy director and community college faculty. I eventually found myself in the role of education director at a Long Beach, California trade school. I soon found that I probably wasn't hired because of my academic acumen but more for my ability to manage a pretty tough big-city school that a large education company had recently acquired. We had a significant number of students who were from some of the most notorious Los Angeles area gangs. Our attrition numbers were affected by students getting shot on the mean streets where they lived. One of our morning classes only had one student in the group who wasn't on probation or parole. Fights were common when I first got there. It wasn't pretty. But we soon brought things under control by helping an excellent group of outstanding building trades subject matter experts who were in front of the classes to become excellent teachers as well. Most of them had the natural talent but no one had ever taken the time to share the 'big picture' or provide the guidance they needed to refine their techniques.

My final day at the campus, I was the last person in the building, or so I thought, and I was locking up for the night. I heard footsteps coming down the dark hallway. A large man approached me who was obviously no stranger to hard times and had probably seen his share of action on the street.

"Wait," he said.

I was fully prepared for the worst in the event this was not going to be a positive contact. Downtown Long Beach had big city crime issues and I didn't immediately know who this person might be.

The man called me by name and hugged me. He said, "I know this is your last day, and I wanted to tell you something. I used to be a loser, now I'm an electrician," he said. "I almost quit. I wanted to thank you for that advice you gave me … I stuck it out."

I didn't ask what advice it was, and I didn't remember talking to him before. It was a pretty big school and moved at a hectic pace. I'm guessing I shared the usual words of encouragement I freely used with students to keep them motivated and feeling like we were on a shared journey to a better future. This student and I shared an emotional moment. I was moved by the pride he took in his life changing accomplishments. I think most teachers and staff in the career education field have those moments from time to time. It is difficult not to. You can't turn everyone's life around, but you can turn *a lot of lives around*, lives that would have likely been ignored by other types of educational institutions.

My commitment to career education is unyielding. Like the police department, from where I came from, the career education field is easily maligned by those not familiar with it, but so very necessary. Also, like policing, there is a commitment within the career education ranks to constantly seek and attain improvement and positive change.

I hope you find our thoughts, experiences, and suggested we share in this book to be helpful.

Daniel Byram

CHAPTER 1 - THE PRIVATE POST-SECONDARY CAMPUS

"Never before has it been as crucial for those of us in career college education to highlight how important emerging trends and innovation are to our future success. The timing of this book comes as higher education is facing unforeseen challenges and provides a guide to help faculty take their creative ideas to improve real-life student learning. Career Colleges are experts at being nimble and open to change and this allows for real-time improvements focused on student outcomes."

Susan Pailet-Compton, EdD, Chief Academic Officer, American Career College

Introduction

This section will introduce you to the typical structure, methods, and systems involved in running a private post-secondary education campus. This will seem quite different than the traditional educational environment you've experienced. We will discuss the roles of key campus staff, students, and schedules. We will also introduce topics that are elaborated on throughout the book. This chapter will provide a context for your responsibilities inside the classroom, thus making it easier to adapt to your new role and become a highly successful classroom instructor.

Key Terms

- Accreditation
- Adult Students
- Advisory Board
- Career Education
- Campus President

- Campus Roles
- Enrollment
- Financial aid
- For-profit
- Mission
- Non-profit
- Schedules
- Traditional
- Workforce preparation and employment

Congratulations, you are hired!

Welcome to private postsecondary education. In this book we will focus on those of you who are going to be teaching at a career school for the first time and those experienced faculty who are ready to improve and refresh their skills. For the purposes of our journey, we identify career schools as private postsecondary institutions in which the primary focus is developing a skilled and successful workforce in the community.

You were recruited because you are a subject matter expert (SME), rather than a trained educator or academic, although you might be that too. You are probably reading this book to help you successfully translate your professional expertise into a successful classroom presentation where you will turn unskilled students into employable workers. But in order to be successful, you need to know how to teach, handle students, and how to work effectively with other faculty and campus leaders. You also need to know how the institution operates and the nuances of the business of a postsecondary institution that might be a non-profit or for-profit business. As a practitioner you might very likely have government or business experience in addition to your subject matter expertise. Teachers are naturally curious people, and they like to know how things work, particularly in vocational fields. We hope to address your questions and concerns in this book.

A teacher in a career school will be engaging in an experience that is similar in some ways, but remarkably different in others, to their counterparts at State Universities, Private non-profit Universities, and Community Colleges.

In a career school, you will often find very tightly developed lessons and schedules. You are a practitioner or expert in the field in which you are teaching, so you will be very familiar with the content. Your job will be to make the content interesting to the students, help them develop an appreciation for the importance of each new skill and each piece of knowledge they receive, and to guide them to become effective practitioners at an entry level position. In other words, they will become hard working contributors to society with a bright future should they embrace and successfully navigate the challenge.

The lessons for each course are development by SME instructors, like you, with input from employers and in consideration of accreditors and industry standards of practice. The resulting lessons are highly structured, and the schedules are tight. There is not a lot of room for pontification and 'war stories' unless they map directly to the objectives of the learning. Students must attend class, be focused, and actively participate in the lessons to succeed. It's fast paced, and it's designed that way for a reason. That reason is to get the student trained and to work as fast as possible without sacrificing the quality of the learning.

Unlike other post-secondary institutions, your school is evaluated by its accreditor and possibly the state (more on those later) on how many students complete the program, go to work in a job for which they were trained, and stay employed. There are three words that describe the mission of a private post-secondary institution, and those words are jobs, jobs, jobs.

Your students often come to your classroom as adults who were not successful in high school or dropped out of community college or the university. Most of them will be low income, have children, and many have work experience in an unskilled labor market. The students want more out of life, but they require the structure, discipline, and focus of a typical private post-secondary program, otherwise, they may be doomed to fail again. They also need a job, so the faster they can complete their program and get to work the better.

So, there you are… a new teacher, in front of a classroom of adults who have no patience with traditional learning institutions, who need a good job with a real future, and who want to be successful but don't know how. That is your challenge. You mission is to get them there. We will give you the details on the "who what when where why" and how as we explore your new opportunity in this book.

Private Career Education

Private career education is an important component of the U.S. Education system.

Compared to traditional private and public universities, career schools offer more relaxed entrance or admissions requirements. This is done in order to attract students who may be more successful in the pursuit of higher education in a more structured and supportive environment which is what career schools offer.

As adults, career students typically have multiple obligations such as children, jobs and caring for other relatives. Most fall into a "zero family contribution" on the federal financial aid scale, meaning they must fully finance their schooling through a job, student financial aid, or loans. They don't have it easy. While brimming with potential, career students typically lack a strong academic orientation in high school or in previous college attempts. Career schools exist to provide opportunity to these students to be trained in their area of interest and in an area of ready employability, thus improving overall access to education with its attendance, financial aid, and personal benefits.

Student attendance at ALL accredited postsecondary schools, public and private, is funded through federal Title IV money (government grants and guaranteed student loans), private loans and grants, veterans benefits and cash payments.

Compared to Public Postsecondary Education

Unlike its public education counterpart, private career education is very restrictive and highly regulated. For example, private career education is measured by completion and placement rates that must be met in order to remain accredited. Meeting required completion and employment rates with the career school population is a significant challenge for every campus. Traditional colleges and universities are not responsible for reporting and meeting the completion and placement standards that are applied to career schools.

Of course, career and traditional schools are characterized by other differences such as in physical facilities, in student services (sports, social events), in the campus relationship with its external communities, and in the faculty and staff responsibilities and focus.

Curriculum content is generally the same in public and private sectors, but the creation, scheduling and oversight is much different. Career schools must be very customer- (i.e., student)-accommodating to appeal to a high-risk student population. There is generally very little focus on liberal arts and general education content involved in career schools as the mission is to train students in a timely manner and get them to work. Associate degrees have limited general education focus, while diploma and certificate do not include general education topics per se.

The mission of public institutions is quite different. With a few exceptions, career schools do not have sports teams, fraternities and sororities, or social events other than local campus events and activities focused on that campus' students and their families.

Distinct Missions

There's a need for both public and private post-secondary institutions in the education marketplace. While you will encounter a broad range of opinions as to the pros and cons of each type of institution, it is important to remember that each enjoy a unique mission and appeal to different populations. Each serves a valuable purpose in the bigger world.

Students will select a school that is the best match for their individual goals.

Comparison of Mission Statements – Career Schools versus Traditional Colleges

Most businesses and non-profit organizations have a mission statement that defines their purpose and their target constituency. The Mission Statement exists to focus the organization on their main business or activities and as a touch point for strategic planning, growing, and allocation of resources. As a working professional, you may be familiar with the Mission Statement of your employer organization.

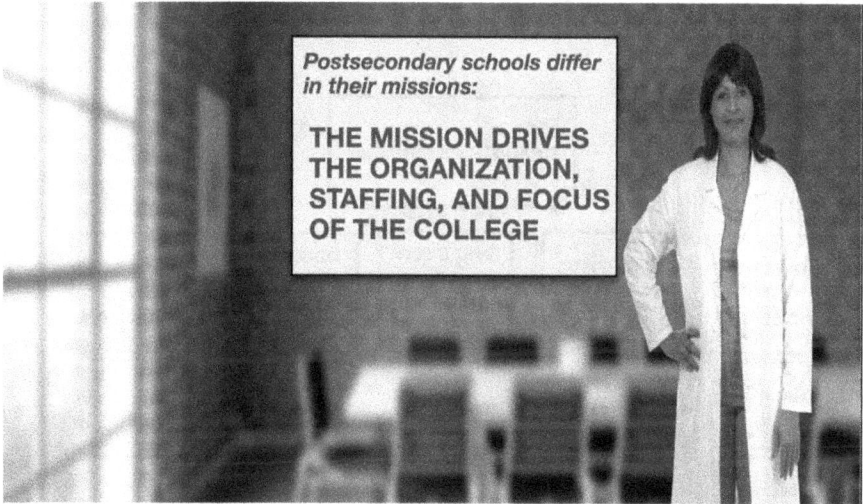

Postsecondary schools differ in their missions:

THE MISSION DRIVES THE ORGANIZATION, STAFFING, AND FOCUS OF THE COLLEGE

One way to understand the various purposes of postsecondary institutions is through a comparison of their mission statements, as follows:

- **Mission Statement: California State University**

  To advance and extend knowledge, learning and culture, especially throughout California. To provide opportunities for individuals to develop intellectually, personally and professionally.

- **Mission Statement: Sinclair Community College**

Find the need and endeavor to meet it by providing high quality, accessible learning as a college of and for the community.

- **Mission Statement: The University of Notre Dame**

  The University of Notre Dame is a Catholic academic community of higher learning, animated from its origins by Congregation of Holy Cross. The University is dedicated to the pursuit and sharing of truth for its own sake.

- **Mission Statement: UEI College**

  We prepare students for employment by providing industry-relevant education and training within a positive, caring and supportive environment.

Key Campus Roles

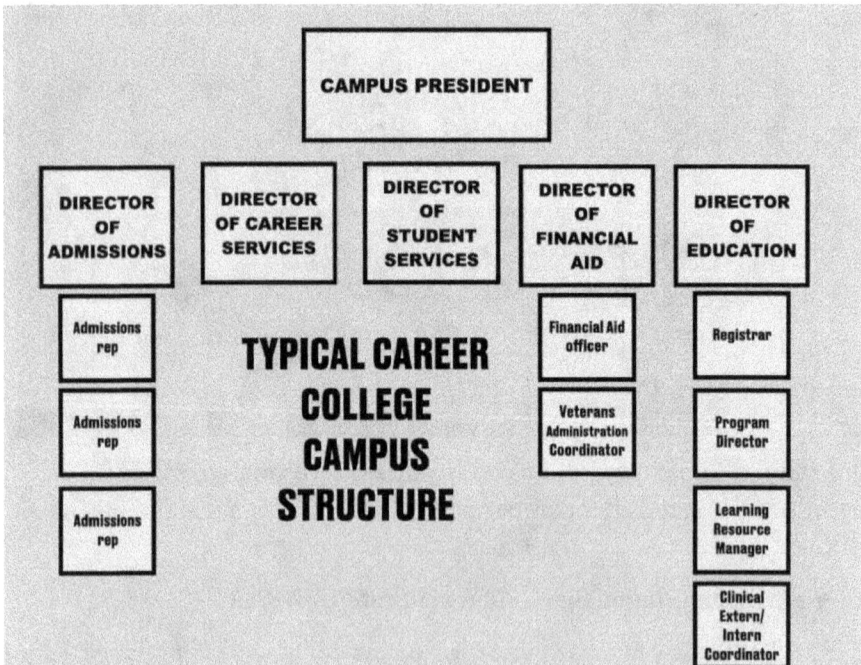

In most private postsecondary schools, you have five key roles that represent the on-site functions of the campus. These roles are Campus President (or Director) who is the Chief Executive, The Director of Education, who is the academic officer, the Director of Enrollment who recruits new students, the Finance Director who helps students find funding for their education, the Director of Career Services who completes the loop and helps students prepare for and find entry level employment. We will look at each of these roles individually. This structure might differ from institution to institution but at the local campus level, this is a very common structure.

Campus President

This is the person who probably approved your being hired. The campus president overseas all of the other directors and commands school operations including student issues, personnel, budget, and other executive functions.

The campus president is the face of the school and will set the tone for the operation. If the school is part of a larger organization, the campus president will report to the corporate leadership, private owners, or a non-profit board depending on the organization type and structure.

Director of Education (DOE)

The Director of education manages the school's academic functions. This role is critical to establishing the quality of the teachers, education, classroom operations, and compliance with regulatory requirements.

The DOE will work with the other directors to make sure classes are scheduled and filled, students are in attendance, and lessons are being delivered according to accreditation and state approvals.

Director of Enrollment

The enrollment director manages the recruitment of students and walks each new student through the process of enrolling in class up through completion of the first week of school. The enrollment director matches the student's interests with the appropriate program. Enrollment representatives report to the director of enrollment.

Director of Career Services

The director of career services will work with students to prepare them for competition in the job market. The director will provide guidance in resume writing, interviewing skills, and workplace etiquette. The director will also work with potential employers through an advisory board to verify that the curriculum delivered matches the demands of the workplace.

Other Campus Roles

Three other campus positions have frequent interactions with faculty are Director of Student Services, Registrar and Program Director.

Director of Student Services (DOSS)

The director of student services oversees the extracurricular needs of students to help ensure their success from day one through graduation. This includes referral to social agencies to secure solutions for personal and family problems, intervention on disciplinary and attendance issues, and creating a sense of community throughout the campus through student and staff participation in social and community events. Instructors refer students to the DOSS for issues that do not come under their teaching responsibilities or for students with continuing disciplinary issues.

Registrar

The registrar is the custodian of student records which includes documentation of attendance, grades and completion of requisite courses and other requirements dictated by regulation and school policy. The registrar typically reports to the Director of Education or the Campus President.

Program Director

For each program offered, institutional and programmatic accreditors require program supervision by an industry-specific professional with specified academic credentials, industry experience and demonstrated teaching proficiency. According to the teaching assignment, instructors are assigned to a program director who is their director supervisor and the first line go-to campus resource for all issues.

Other Positions

Larger organizations may employ additional education staff to lead specialized functions such as Curriculum Development, Institutional Research and Assessment, Distance Education and Accreditation Compliance. Very large institutions typically employ such individuals in a headquarters environment. As a faculty member and SME, you might have the opportunity to interact with these individuals and functions in your responsibilities outside the classroom.

The Advisory Board

The last piece of the campus organization puzzle we will discuss in this chapter is the advisory board. The advisory board is a group representing local employers. They routinely meet with the campus directors in events organized by the Director of Career Services. The board provides critical input to matters of interest to the school including, but not limited to:

- New skills required by employers
- Hiring outlook
- Curriculum analysis
- Program analysis
- Professional insights

- Feedback on students who have been hired

This board is the guiding light to the future success of the institution.

> **If students can't get jobs, then some part of the operation is not functioning properly. Conversely, if employers are competing to hire your students, then the operation is heading in the right direction.**

As a subject matter expert, you will likely be invited to attend Advisory Board meetings to facilitate and add to the discussion about employer needs and to help interpret and evaluate advisory board input for administrators who are responsible for evaluating, planning, creating, and revising programs.

The Schedule

The schedule at a career school might seem intense at first. But remember, the goal is to get a student trained in the requisite skills and professional behaviors in their targeted job as quickly as possible and get them to the employment market. Most campuses offer multiple variations of a schedule each term, and typically a student will be offered a choice to attend classes during the morning, or afternoon, or evening for four or five days a week for the duration of their program. Thus, students can select a schedule that best suits their personal preference in accommodating family, work or other obligations. Generally, students attend only one full-time class per term.

Certificate programs are of short duration, diplomas are usually around nine months, and associate degree programs are around eighteen months. These are very broad generalizations. Many programs, certificates, and diplomas have specific requirements for time commitments in lecture and lab hours as well as externship, internship and other practicum experiences. These time frames are dictated by states, the Department of Education, and institutional and programmatic accreditors to ensure students get the adequate amount and proportion of time in each of the curriculum components.

As a teacher, or other staff member, your schedule will be determined by the school to support the term's calendar and student schedules.

Students generally progress through their program in cohorts or in wheels. Cohorts are a discreet group that starts and finishes together. This linear model strictly defines what courses are to be taken first, second and so on – including pre-requisites such as medical terminology before anatomy and physiology or evidence collection before criminal investigation. A wheel is a cycle of courses (making up a program) that can be started at any time in any given course in the program. That means that a new student can start their program in any class and a new student might be attending with students who are about to finish their program. In a wheeled program, classes are self-contained and there are no pre-requisites for most of the courses.

The primary advantage of a cohort or wheeled schedule is students being able to start a program precisely when they are ready as start dates are available monthly on a continuous basis; and should a student be compelled to stop out for a period of time due to work or family commitments, s/he can start back up almost immediately (monthly) when ready. This is another way private career schools help get students trained and to the job market expeditiously.

The Students

After you meet the students, you might notice that they are older and more experienced than the typical high school graduate who is going to the state university.

Career school students may have families, a job as an unskilled laborer, and ambition to do more with their life. Some will not be able to succeed in the traditional education environment. They will be grateful for your help, but also quick to call you out if they disagree or don't believe what you are telling them. It can be challenging.

As you go through the chapters you will find information about adult learning and how to best teach in the adult learner environment. Remember, don't make assumptions. Students are in a space that they are not necessarily comfortable or familiar with. It is easy to assume that they know what you expect of them and what they are supposed to do. There has to be a clear understanding of accountability that is evenly and fairly used with all students. Balance that with avoiding any appearance of being judgmental or condescending. Adults do not react well to being treated as children.

You will find this balancing act difficult at first but by providing consistency in your dealings with all students, you will help your students understand the rigorous demands of learning and working in the real world.

Achieving success in this environment can be very rewarding, and many instructors have found it improves their other professional and personal relationships.

Summary

Teaching in a career school is a unique experience with interesting opportunities and challenges. Private postsecondary, or career education, schools offer an alternative to traditional education paths for non-traditional students. These include quicker programs with more hands-on learning that lead to the entry level job market.

There are critical leadership positions at each campus with some common but also discreet responsibilities. These leaders include the president and the directors of education, recruitment, finance, and career services. As an instructor, your understanding and coordination with these key positions will make your job easier and enhance students' experience and success.

The advisory board plays a key role in the vision and direction of each school. Jobs and careers are the primary focus of most private post-secondary education institutions and they work in partnership with their advisory boards.

A career school is the logical choice for an adult student whose goal is to obtain an education and job within the most efficient and effective time frame.

CHAPTER 2 - CAREER EDUCATION SECTOR OVERVIEW

"For those of us who love to change the lives of financially disadvantaged individuals in a safe, caring, experiential, and engaging learning community while making a meaningful contribution to society, few occupations match what we achieve daily in post-secondary career education. As educators who prepare students for high demand careers in fast growing industries, career college professionals serve a population of students who have historically and traditionally been under-prepared and under-represented. Career education doesn't replace traditional postsecondary education; we complement the sector by offering much needed training to prepare America's future workers. It's truly an honor to have the opportunity to train our students and help them build futures they can be proud of."

Fardad Fateri, PhD, President and Chief Executive Officer International Education Corporation

Introduction

In this section we will explore the career education world and take what CEOs refer to as the 30,000-foot view of how career schools fit into the higher education system, some of the unique features of career schools, and how career schools and students enhance the workforce.

Colleges took hold in the United States early on as religious groups established universities to train ministers, already common in Europe. Schools to train medical doctors and children of wealthy families in the liberal arts followed. A college degree became an important component of the American Dream for the general population when young men were transitioning from farming to other professions in the early 20th century.

U.S. Land Grant universities originally specialized in agriculture, to improve the efficiency of the burgeoning food industry in the U.S. and abroad, and engineering which produced graduates to lead the looming technical revolution. Black Land-Grant Universities, now referred to as HBUC, formed to train teachers and foreign students who returned home to improve farming and production. Later came state university systems and community colleges, each with their particular missions to educate the masses. Eventually offering more programs, these universities became beacons of middle-class values supporting young people, mostly men in the early days, transitioning to white-collar occupations.

Key Terms

- Career Colleges
- Certification
- Career and Technical Education (CTE)
- Postsecondary education
- Standard Aptitude Tests
- Trade Schools
- Vocational Colleges

College Enrollment

There are approximately 20 million students enrolled in US colleges according to latest data from the National Center for Education Statistics. That number is the equivalent to the population of the greater Los Angeles area, about three-fourths of the entire population of Texas, or about half of the United States population between the ages of 18 and 30. By any measure, that is a lot of people.

When discussing college, one readily thinks of the traditional state university, the local community college, or even big-name private colleges and universities such as Harvard and Purdue. Of course, this is not the whole story. Those institutions do not represent the entire spectrum of higher education. Of the 20 million US college students, approximately 15 million of them attend big, or big name, colleges and universities. The remaining 5 million, or about 25% of college students, attend private colleges. Of these private colleges, about 2 million attend private for-profit colleges, often referred to as Career Colleges.

Estimated Number of Postsecondary Institutions and College Enrollments 2020
National Center for Education Statistics, 2018

	All Post-secondary Institutions	Public Universities	Public Community Colleges	Private Not for Profit Colleges	Private For Profit Colleges
Number of institutions	6100	1900	900	1800	1500
Number of Students	21,000,000	10 M	5.0 M	4.0 M	2.0 M[*1]

*[*1] Enrollments at private for-for profit colleges, commonly referred to as Career Education and Technical Education institutions, are approximately half degree-seeking and half diploma-seeking (less than two years of study) students.*

Additional Sources:

Career Education Colleges and Universities, 2020
Inside Higher Education, June 2018
Association of American Colleges and Universities, 2019

At nearly 10% of the total college system, career colleges are an important and enduring part of the United States college system.

That a college degree is a ticket of sorts to a better life has proven to be true, at least from a financial perspective. Over the lifetime of a career, it is estimated that the holder of a college degree will earn nearly $1 million more in salary. And, unemployment rates are historically lower for college graduates, often as much as one half that of high school graduates. College graduates are a major contributor to the U.S. Labor Force which requires skilled workers, beyond the high school graduate, at all levels of the organization – i.e., blue and white collar.

AVERAGE SALARY BY EDUCATION LEVEL

FROM SMARTASSET I AMELIA JOSEPHSON I MAY 15, 2018

Education Level	Average Annual Salary	Average Unemployment Rate
No HS Diploma	$ 25,636	8%
High School	$ 35,256	5.4%
Some College	$ 38,376	5%
Associates Degree	$ 41,496	3.8%
Bachelor's Degree	$ 59,124	2.8%

Career Colleges

When you hear the term Career Education, what comes to mind? Where does Career Education fit within our education system? Why is the distinction made between Career Education and other types of formal training and education?

Career Education refers to a specific sector of the postsecondary education field. Our education system is segmented by Primary Education (generally defined as "K-8"), Secondary Education ("High School"), and Postsecondary Education (i.e., after, or post-High School), or in other words, college. Career education colleges, most of which are organized as for-profit institutions, are a significant part of the US college system.

Career colleges train students, generally for entry-level employment, in specified technical jobs in medical services, construction trades, automotive and aviation repair, culinary, fashion design, cosmetology, information technology, security, and in business administration as receptionists, administrative assistants, bookkeepers, and other clerical functions.

"More students than ever are opting for a FOUR-YEAR degree. But trade jobs account for 54% of the labor force. There will be 3.5 million jobs to be filled over next 10 years. 2 million of these jobs will go unfilled due to the skills gap. The [current generation of traditional college grads] is struggling to bridge the gap between what they learned and the [employment] opportunities. Trade jobs don't require massive debt, and don't require four years of study. They require the attainment of skills that are actually in demand." **Mike Rowe, Dirty Jobs, Discovery Channel** *and Somebody's Gotta Do It, CNN*

The rise of career schools followed the end of World War II with a corresponding rise in homebuilding and manufacturing to support GIs who were starting families and transitioning to the civilian workforce. Many of these veterans, older and more focused perhaps than a typical 18-year-old high school graduate, wanted job training faster than traditional 4-year colleges could provide. A second wave of interest came about later in the twentieth century due to the increase in skills and technology demands of many jobs and new and emerging jobs in the technology field per se. Interest in training has continued to increase with the specialization and corresponding certification for jobs in fields such as healthcare and information technology. Adding to the increased interest in post-secondary education are the competitive hurdles posed by industries such as criminal justice and business where a college diploma is often the key to a promotion or getting hired in the first place.

Career Colleges are sometimes referred to as Vocational Colleges, Technical Education, or Trade Schools. By any name, these schools focus on practical or skills training. In career colleges, students are trained in a specific set of skills leading to a specific job.

College Admissions

Generally, admissions requirements in a career college are relaxed when compared to more traditional academic institutions such as a state or private universities. For example, career colleges do not require the submission of scores from standard aptitude tests such as the Scholastic Aptitude Test (SAT) or the American College Testing (ACT) and will accept a lower high school grade point average than a traditional college. Many career school enrollees come back to school with years of work and life experience, unlike the 18-year-old traditional college freshman.

Most career schools do not require personal or professional references.

Nonetheless, the vast majority of career schools do require the successful completion of an entrance exam or assessment to ensure that potential enrollees possess adequate reading, writing, and math skills necessary to successfully complete their program of interest. One example is the Wonderlic Cognitive Ability Test. Wonderlic test results are correlated to success in a range of different occupations. As such, schools typically set different achievement scores on the Wonderlic depending on the program in which the student wishes to be enrolled.

Admission to a career school requires a high school diploma or its equivalent such as the General Education Development Test (GED).

Upon successful completion of a career school program, a graduate is awarded a Diploma or Certificate.

Over the last 15-20 years, an increasing number of career schools offer educational programs leading to an Associate Degree. This trend addresses growing requirements in some employment fields which require increased technical and interpersonal skills even in entry-level or to advance to mid-level positions. Examples include medical fields such Surgical Technology, Nursing and Radiology Tech, all of which are continuously impacted by technological advancements and increased patient diversity driving the need for more and different skills. By definition, Associate Degree programs are more academic than certificate or diploma programs and require general education and elective course components. The length and composition of any career college program is reflective of the requirements of the employment market and the credential required.

Career School Demographics

The personal characteristics of career college students often vary greatly and meaningfully from their traditional counterparts. Career college students are typically older. The majority have little or no family financial contribution to the cost of their education. Many have children. Most have jobs. They do not live "on campus" as they navigate the many hurdles to program completion and graduation. However, they do recognize that a college education is a means to career employment and to greater financial success than with no college education at all. They are classic adult learners who bring experience and motivation to the classroom and who want it fast and relevant.

Comparison of Traditional and Career College Students on Admissions Factors

	Traditional College Student	Career College Student
Average Age	20-21	28
Entrance Exam	Yes (SAT/ACT)	Yes (Wonderlic, Compass, American College Test)
References Required	Yes	No
Degree Seeking	Bachelors, Masters, Doctorate	Certificate, Diploma, Associates, Bachelors
Expected Family Contribution (EFC) per Title IV regulations FAFSA calculation	$3000-4,000 for one year w/ Household AGI of $50,000; Often, wealthy families' EFC exceeds the cost of tuition	Often students are emancipated, and EFC is zero
Typical Profile	Single, seeking professional career, May be exploring multiple career options, Percent of female enrollment 40%	Parents (51%), Employed (20 hours), Seeking a specific career, Percent of female enrollment 55%

Sources: National Center for Education Statistics (NCES) 2018, EDUCATIONDATA.ORG 2020

Summary

Career education provides efficient and high-quality preparation for those who wish to join the workforce as rapidly as possible, be promoted, or need to develop special skills or knowledge to retain a job.

Arguably, two of the better measures of college success are the relative employment and earning rates of college graduates over high school graduates. In general, studies show that as college enrollment and completion go up, earnings increase, and unemployment rates go down. A Georgetown University study completed about five years ago found that college graduates, compared to high school grads, earn about $1.0 Million more over their lifetime.

As each increment of college completion (certificate, diploma, associates) results in higher earnings and lower unemployment rates, we know that the Career education space is an essential and effective component of the US educational system.

CHAPTER 3 - FACULTY ROLES AND RESPONSIBILITIES

"For all faculty involved in adult learning, the adage, "Be the guide on the side, not the sage on the stage," is the guiding principle in establishing a classroom that promotes introspection, critical thinking, and genuine learning. As a result, students are able to enhance their career viability while fostering self-worth."

Tom Carras, MSEd, Lt. Col., USMC, retired. Undergraduate and graduate instructor and Senior Faculty at the University of Phoenix for over 25 years.

Introduction

You came to teach!

It's going to be fun!

And you will learn so much!

Clearly the main role of faculty is to teach students. This involves not only being an experienced professional in the teaching area, but also performing a number of other related roles and responsibilities. In addition to preparing for and delivering the course, every college requires faculty to perform at least a few bits of administrative work. This work includes taking attendance, recording and submitting grades, participating in professional development and in-service activities, and interacting with administrative staff. Other responsibilities such as counseling students, overseeing practicum sites, supervising externs, serving on advisory boards, or writing curriculum may be assigned depending on the institution.

Faculty responsibilities are governed in part by accreditation. Accreditation is classified as either Institutional or Programmatic.

While being accredited is self-imposed, in other words voluntary, most postsecondary institutions find it highly desirable. Accreditation measures the quality of a school or program against a documented set of standards determined by membership institutions, accreditation staff and their board of commissioners.

Students, employers, parents, and other constituents look to a college's performance on accreditation standards to determine its suitability according to their objectives. Inasmuch as teaching and learning is at the core of any college's mission and vision, it makes sense that accreditation standards would address faculty issues such as qualifications, teaching assignments, training and development, and job responsibilities.

This section will explain qualifications necessary to teach and other common administrative responsibilities associated with teaching at the college level.

Key Terms

- Qualifications
- Subject Matter Expert
- Administrative Duties
- Licensing
- Professional Development
- In-Service
- Accreditation and Compliance
- Faculty Qualifications

What are the standards?

Institutional accrediting bodies who oversee career colleges set standards for faculty hiring and teaching assignments. These standards define requisite academic preparation as well as practical work experience. Typically, an instructor is required to have academic credentials (i.e., a diploma or degree from an accredited institution) in the teaching area at one level higher than the academic diploma or degree to be awarded the graduating students. For example, the instructor teaching in a program which awards a diploma, must have an associate degree; a faculty teaching in a program that awards an associate degree must hold at least a bachelor's degree, and so on. However, some accreditors set the higher degree requirement only for the Program Director who supervises the program and its faculty. States and programmatic accreditors may have even higher degree standards in some programs, especially in nursing and other healthcare professions.

In addition to the academic credential, most accrediting agencies require the instructor to have a minimum of three years' work experience in the teaching area.

At most institutions, instructors teaching a general education course in a degree-granting program must hold the minimum of a master's degree with 18 semester credits or 15 quarter credits in the subject matter. Work experience, which is more difficult to match in the general education area, must accumulate to a minimum three years in a related field. For instance, a communications instructor may satisfy the work experience requirement through employment as a marketing assistant, a lawyer, a published author, a copywriter at a radio station, as a Human Resources staff member, or through a combination thereof.

Program Directors

The Program Directors are part faculty, part administrator and part manager. They are typically required to hold a degree one level above the program as well as three year's work experience in the field, AND a minimum of three year's teaching experience, and supervisory experience.

You were screened in the employment process for the requisite academic and experiential qualifications as dictated by your Campus accreditor. Requirements vary somewhat among institutional and programmatic accreditors, as well as by states. The table below provides a link to the leading national accreditors overseeing career schools, all of which outline faculty requirements in their Standards of Accreditation.

Accreditor	Abbreviation	Web Address	Location
Accrediting Bureau of Health Education Schools	ABHES	www.abhes.org	Falls Church, Virginia
Accrediting Commission of Career Schools and Colleges	ACCSC	www.accsc.org	Arlington, Virginia
Accrediting Council for Independent Colleges and Schools	ACICS	www.acics.org	Washington, D.C.
Accrediting Council for Continuing Education and Training	ACCET	www.accet.org	Washington, D.C.
Distance Education Accrediting Commission	DEAC	www.deac.org	Washington, D.C.
Higher Learning Commission	HLC	www.hlcommission.org	Chicago, Illinois
Western Association of Schools and Colleges	WASC	www.acswasc.org	Burlingame, California
Council on Occupational Education	COE	www.council.org	Atlanta, Georgia

Continued accreditation is predicated on your Campus compliance with all its Standards of Accreditation. Your accreditor's faculty requirements are listed in detail in the Standards of Accreditation, Faculty Section of their Accreditation Manual which may be accessed online at the accreditor's website. By way of example, see the Appendix to this chapter for the ABHES standards related to faculty.

The Faculty File

In the course of the hiring process, a faculty has responsibility to submit a request for forwarding their academic transcripts and to provide a summary of professional work experience to the Campus. Foreign transcripts may qualify an applicant to teach; however, the transcript must be officially evaluated for academic equivalency by an agency recognized by the U.S. Department of Education to perform such evaluations.

All schools keep an academic file on each faculty which contains official transcripts of academic degrees, substantiation of work experience, evidence of ongoing professional development and in-service participation, copies of required licensures and certifications, as well as any awards or other acknowledgments that document the instructor's qualifications to teach in the courses assigned.

Accreditation prohibits the college from assigning a faculty until all required documentation of academic and experiential work is provided to the college. An organization's failure to evidence required documentation of the instructor's qualifications will be identified in an accreditation team visitor's review of each faculty file and will subject the organization to a citation for failure to meet the accreditation standard. Such citations are considered serious and must be resolved at once. In addition to accreditation concerns, the teaching assignment of faculty without the requisite academic or work qualifications may subject the college to legal liability.

Faculty must cooperate fully with providing the college the required documentation to teach prior to taking a course assignment, as well as providing the college with yearly updates to professional development activity, licensures, additional academic coursework, etc.

Subject Matter Expert

A faculty with academic preparation and work experience in a specified area is referred to as a Subject Matter Expert (SME). An SME is someone with deep understanding of the teaching area gained through the accumulation of academic credits, work experience, participation in professional development activities or associations, or who has completed speaking engagements or professional writings.

Career Colleges employ SMEs as instructors to ensure students are exposed not only to the theoretical knowledge in their desired field of employment, but also to learn other professional and practical aspects of the career field. SMEs are critical to an optimal learning experience, especially for adult learners whose goal is to gain practical workplace and professional employment skills.

Being an SME may qualify an instructor to participate in curriculum development initiatives for the college.

SMEs may be contacted by publishers to participate in development or evaluation of learning materials.

Accreditation agencies engage SMEs to participate in the development of program standards, to develop model curriculum outlines, to evaluate program performance and to train and advise member organizations and their staff and faculty.

Licensing and Continuing Education

As teachers, we subscribe to lifelong learning. Thus, we have an interest in continuing to learn and grow professionally beyond our initial college and early work experiences. In fact, college regulators require it!

Licensing

Some professional organizations and state regulators require certain professionals to not only hold a specified academic credential, but to be evaluated on their knowledge and skills through third-party standardized testing in order to obtain a license to work in the designated field. These include doctors, nurses, K-12 teachers, certified public accountants, attorneys, and others. To become a registered nurse (R.N.), upon graduation from an accredited and state-approved nursing program, one must pass the standardized National Council Licensure Examination (NCLEX). Similarly, an attorney must obtain a license to practice law through successful completion of the State Bar Examination. Most states require college graduates who wish to teach in the K-12 system to pass the PRAXIS exam. And so on. Other administrative requirements must be fulfilled to obtain licensure in these fields (e.g., background checks, fingerprinting). Only when graduates have successfully passed the licensing exam and successfully navigated other administrative requirements, a license to work is granted.

A professional who is required to have a license in the field to practice must hold an up-to-date license to teach in the field. Where a license is required to work in the field, and therefore qualify you to teach, a current license must be evidenced in the faculty file.

Continuing Education

In order for specified professionals to maintain their licenses, regulators require them to complete a stated number of hours of professional development coursework or other qualifying learning activity over a specified period of time. This activity is commonly referred to as Continuing Education. This is true for nurses and other medical professionals, K-12 teachers, and attorneys, to name a few. For example, attorneys who are actively practicing law in California must take a minimum of 25 hours continuing legal education every three years. In Ohio, a registered nurse must take 24 hours of continuing education during each two-year licensure period and at least one of the hours must be related to Chapter 4723 of the Nurse Practice Code (re: Scope of Practice and Professional Boundaries). And, in some cases, especially where there is emerging interest or legal concerns, the professional organization representing the state's interest dictates an actual area of learning that must be attended such as Sexual Harassment, Diversity, certain medical procedures (e.g., Intravenous Therapy), and so on.

Professionals failing to fulfill continuing education or other administrative requirements risk suspension or loss of their license to practice in the field and would not be qualified to teach in the specified field under the standards of accreditation.

Certification

Where students are required to obtain certification from a third-party testing agency in order to work in the field, a campus may require their instructors to maintain industry certification as a condition of employment. Where a campus program is programmatically accredited (e.g., AHIMA, CoARC, ARCST), an instructor in the substantive subject matter or, at a minimum, the Program Director would be required to hold the certification. The Campus will communicate any such requirements to the applicant in the hiring process.

Professional Development and In-Service Training

Professional Development

Institutional and programmatic accreditors require instructors to participate in professional development activities throughout their career as an instructor.

Professional Development is required to increase one's knowledge and performance in the subject matter of assigned teaching. The idea is to ensure that an SME maintains currency in the teaching area, especially as they devote more of their professional time to teaching in lieu of practicum work in the field. Qualifying activities include attendance at professional conferences, completing additional academic or professional coursework, participation in speaking engagements, volunteering in professional activities, and completing activities for the upkeep of professional licenses and Certification through Continuing Education or completion of practicum experience.

Professional development may be conducted within the college environment but is more commonly completed outside the organization as it would be cost-and-operationally-prohibitive for the College for provide adequate professional development opportunities for the range of teaching (subject matter) areas across all programs. For example, professional development for a healthcare professional varies from that of a criminal justice instructor.

Colleges are required to budget for expenses to promote faculty professional development. Budget and other professional development parameters should be discussed with your Program Director or Chair, the Director of Education/Academic Dean or Campus President before assuming the activity will be paid for by the College.

In-Service Training

In-Service refers to the accreditor's requirement for the college to provide training to instructors in the practice of teaching and on the continuum of career education issues impacting their teaching responsibilities.

In-Service training is designed to allow professional teachers to meet with their peer group of professional educators, train in new educational techniques and technologies, share best practices, discuss common issues and interests, and keep abreast of developments in the field of education. This allows a very broad range of subjects for consideration when planning In-Service training. Unlike Professional Development, In-Service training is generic and targeted to address all faculty across program disciplines.

Colleges organize In-Service trainings around the topics of Student Outcomes, Regulatory Compliance, Classroom Management, Facilitated Learning, and emerging trends such as Online Delivery, Adaptive Learning, and other educational technologies. Generally In-Service Trainings are conducted several times a year, ideally in-between terms so maximum faculty attendance is achieved.

Some schools invite Program Advisory Board members to attend In-Service Trainings to increase their knowledge of the college and the industry. Also, In-Service Training can be offered to professionals interested in becoming faculty but who have not yet been hired or assigned to teach a course.

Regulators lay out their requirements for In-Service training in the Standards of Accreditation. Instructors are required to attend In-Service training, and the College must provide evidence thereof in the faculty file for review by the accreditor's visiting team.

SUMMARY

While Regulatory Compliance is a professional area of responsibility unto itself, it is critical that you – as faculty – understand some basic concepts as well as the specific requirements related to your qualifications to teach and your fulfillment of compliance-related administrative responsibilities such as attendance taking, assignment of grades, provision of all course hours and lesson plans. Your expertise in this area will grow as you fulfill your teaching responsibilities and attend In-Service training and participate in Professional Development activities.

ADDITIONAL READING

Read and assess Appendix A, the Faculty Standards excerpted from the Accreditation Manual, 18th edition – Accrediting Bureau of Allied Health Schools (ABHES) - Copyright © 2010 Accrediting Bureau of Health Education Schools

CHAPTER 4 – REGULATORY COMPLIANCE

"Higher education is one of the most regulated sectors in America and having faculty that understand the regulatory environment is critical to institutional and student success. Everyone benefits when faculty understand their vital role in regulatory success."

Lisa Parker, J.D., Partner, Husch Blackwell LLP

INTRODUCTION

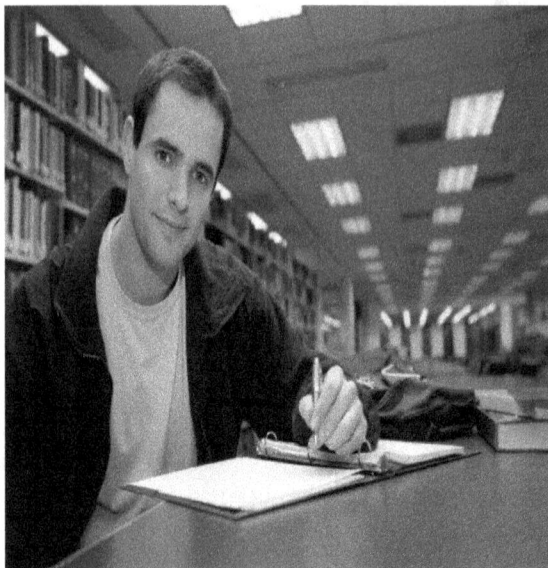

"Is this a good school?"

That's a critical question for students, parents, teachers, employers and other institutional stakeholders in higher education. They want to know if the school offers all it should to ensure optimal teaching and learning, to ensure employable skills and professional development, and that it maintains financial parameters and time frames that will ensure graduates achieve their professional and personal goals. It's a big, complicated discussion that is fraught with emotion, questions and concerns, and hopes and dreams. Many standards and protections exist to ensure that colleges and their employees deliver on their obligations and promises.

The postsecondary education industry is highly regulated. Significant regulators include the U.S. Department of Education (USDOE) and the fifty state governments through education bureaus, boards of nursing, and Occupational Safety and Health Administration (OSHA) offices. Colleges have also developed a system of self-governance through institutional and programmatic accreditors who set professional standards relied upon by the USDOE, students, employers, and the public to continuously guide and evaluate institutional quality and administrative operations of the college.

REGULATORY HIERARCHY IN EDUCATION

ENTITY	GOAL
States	Consumer Protection
Institutional Accreditors	Academic Quality and Financial Aid Gatekeeper
Programmatic Accreditors	Academic Quality, Alignment with Employer Requirements, Graduate Certification
U.S. Department of Education (USDOE)	Oversee Financial Aid, Protect the Treasury and Taxpayers

KEY TERMS

- Copyright
- Department of Education
- Intellectual Property
- Financial Aid
- Institutional Accreditation
- Permissions
- Plagiarism
- Programmatic Accreditation
- Title IV

The U.S. Department of Education and Student Financial Aid

Most regulation emanating from the United States Department of Education (USDOE or DOE) is concerned with the award and distribution of student financial aid in the form of grants, loans and Work-Study funds which help to pay student costs of attending college. Most colleges have an office of student finance which oversees the receipt and distribution of USDOE funds to students. These funds are often referred to as Title IV monies or funds authorized and administered under Title IV of the federal Higher Education Act.

Strict regulations cover required student and parent communications and disclosures, receipt and application of funds, return of unused or excess funds, and issues related to student loan repayment. Student finance offices are subject to regular audits by internal and third party auditors, as well as the USDOE, to ensure compliance with all of the rules covering the receipt, distribution, return and repayment of financial aid funds. The USDOE can restrict distribution of financial aid funds, as well as shut off access to funds altogether, where substantial compliance is not demonstrated by the institution. Most colleges are substantially reliant on federal financial aid to "stay in business;" as such, the detection of serious non-compliance with USDOE regulations is tantamount to shuttering the college.

All financial aid records are subject to an annual audit and to additional periodic on-site audits by the USDOE.

Loss of approval to offer Title IV funds to students is equivilent to "going out of business."

Implications for Instructors

It is not necessary for an instructor to understand all the ins-and-outs of financial aid regulation. But there are some basic principles and requirements related to instructors that are essential to ensuring the institution's compliance with financial aid regulation. The following instructor responsibilities are tied directly to the proper administration of financial aid funds.

The instructor must:

☐ Deliver the exact amount of course hours as outlined in the school catalog, including start and end dates of the course, including start and end times of each class, and including the number, length and timing of breaks during each class meeting. For example: an instructor may not combine all allowable class breaks to let students leave before the published class end time; an instructor may not call off class for the day without a scheduled make up; an instructor may not start a term late or end it early.

☐ Record attendance accurately, including tardiness and leaving early. Specifically, the instructor records but does not approve absences. An absence is an absence is an absence.

☐ Record and submit grades in compliance with the course syllabus and college policy and procedures. For example, you may not enact extra credit or make up scenarios "on the fly" at the end of a course in order for students to improve a grade or pass the course when the planned assignments and examinations were otherwise failed. To be valid, make up and extra credit must be part of the original syllabus which applies to all students and is permitted by college policy.

☐ Change grades only in the case of an error in calculation of assignments or exams.

☐ Refuse to change attendance or grades at the request of a school administrator to appease a student complaint or maintain a student's attendance where no error in record keeping or compliance with the course syllabus or catalog is found.

Upon your employment with the college, an education department administrator will explain the college's academic calendar, course times, attendance policies, and policies related to recording and submitting grades. Compliance with campus policies and procedures in these administrative areas of responsibility will help to ensure your support for the college's regulatory compliance.

Faculty non-compliance with the requirements outlined above jeopardizes the college's and students' eligibility to participate in USDOE financial aid programs and puts the college at risk of student lawsuits and other legal action. In addition, allowing students to bypass course requirements instills poor work and professional habits which could risk students' ability to perform important workplace skills and to maintain satisfactory employment.

Institutional Accreditation

Accreditation seems mysterious and complicated. There's a lot to it, and it takes time to learn it all. While college administrators must be experts on the standards of accreditation, instructors can benefit from understanding just the basics as they begin their teaching responsibilities. We'll keep it simple and relevant here.

Accreditation refers to the valuation of a college against a set of standards developed by peer educators and administrators which, when achieved and consistently followed by the institution, assure students and other stakeholders of an acceptable level of institutional quality. Accreditation standards attempt to drive satisfactory levels of teaching, student learning and professional development, courses and learning materials, as well as insuring faculty, administrators and facilities support defined levels of educational quality as well as the organization's own published mission and vision.

Accreditation standards set parameters (i.e., requirements) for the basic college functions such as Admissions and Enrollment, Delivery of Education Programs, Program Components and Parameters, Student Outcomes, Facilities and Equipment, Faculty Qualifications and Assignments, Distance Education and Student Service requirements such as advisement, academic policy, and job placement assistance.

Upon application for initial accreditation, and for periodic renewed grants of accreditation, a peer review group (i.e., accreditation visiting team) conducts an onsite visit of the institution and its branches to ensure the documented standards of accreditation are being met on a continuing basis. Required reports, to be submitted annually and when triggered by requests such as for new programs and locations, inform the accreditor of student, institutional, and program issues and outcomes. Both visiting team and campus administrative reports are reviewed by the accreditor's elected Board of Commissioners for disposition. Commissioners' disposition could include approval, return for further information, directives for improvement, or sanctions with timeframes for resolution.

Things you need to know about Institutional Accreditation:

1. Accreditation is not required.

2. Accreditation is the gateway to student federal financial aid.

3. An institution must be accredited by a USDOE-recognized accreditor in order for students to receive federal student aid.

4. Accreditors are either of regional or national scope. Six regional accreditors and five national accreditors collectively account for accreditation of the majority of postsecondary institutions. One accreditor (the Distance Education Accrediting Commission or DEAC) exclusively accredits online institutions.

5. The USDOE approves accrediting commissions which apply for and are recognized as reliable authorities on educational quality. Only USDOE-recognized accreditors can provide the gatekeeping function for federal student aid programs.

6. Accreditors conduct non-governmental peer evaluation of institutions and programs to assess academic quality of member institutions.

7. Colleges are subject to the loss of accreditation, and hence participation in federal Title IV programs, if they fail to demonstrate substantial and continued compliance with the standards of accreditation.

Programmatic Accreditation and Certification of Graduates

Many specialized healthcare and information technology jobs require the employee to possess a certification in the field in order to be employed. Certification can only be obtained upon successful completion of a third-party exam which tests for industry-specific knowledge and skills after graduation from the career training program. Programmatic accreditation agencies, which define standards related to levels of skills competency required by employers in certain fields, dictate both the content and skill level to be achieved in a program in order to be certified. Certification is accomplished through standardized testing post-graduation. Often, without the additional certification, the graduate will not be able to be employed in the field for which s/he was trained.

> Note: ABHES is both an institutional and programmatic accreditor for specific allied health programs. As such, if an institution is programmatically accredited by ABHES yet institutionally accredited by another organization, the institution is subject to the full set of ABHES Standards of Accreditation, not just the accredited program. An institution may have both institutional and programmatic accreditation from ABHES, or one or the other.

Different from institutional accreditation which addresses the entire institution and provides a gateway to federal financial aid for students, Programmatic Accreditation is targeted at programs in a college that is already institutionally accredited. Depending on the career field, programmatic accreditation may be just as or even more important than institutional accreditation.

Programmatic accreditors focus on an individual program and help to ensure employers and professional associations that accredited programs are the same from school to school. This is accomplished through having standards set by subject matter and professional experts, through a peer review process similar to institutional accreditors, and through requiring the testing of knowledge and skills post-graduation but prior to employment. Passing of a programmatically accredited assessment exam establishes the test taker's qualifications against professional standards and results in certification.

Certification is prevalent among healthcare professions, with many employers requiring certification for employment (e.g., respiratory therapy, surgical technology). Others indicate certification as a preference (e.g., medical assisting); thus, with all things being equal, the certified graduate will get the job!

Many institutions require their faculty to be certified in the teaching field, especially in the healthcare fields. Where certification is required for employment, it will be required for teaching in the field, at least for the Program Director. Your campus specific requirements for certification are explained in the hiring process.

SELECT PROGRAMATIC ACCREDITORS

Institutional Accreditor	Abbreviation	Website	Location
Commission on Accreditation for Respiratory Care	CoARC	www.coarc.com	Telford, Tennessee
Accreditation Review Council on Education in Surgical Technology and Surgical Assisting	ARC/STSA	www.arcsta.org	Littleton, Colorado
American Association of Medical Assistants	AAMA	www.aama-ntl.org	Chicago, Illinois
American Health Information Management Association	AHIMA	www.ahima.org	Chicago, Illinois
Commission on Dental Accreditation	CODA	www.ada.org	Chicago, Illinois
Pharmacy Technician Accreditation Commission	PTAC	www.acpe-accredit.org or www.ashp.org	Bethesda, Maryland

The process for obtaining programmatic certification is similar to that for institutional accreditation. Requirements are documented in the association's standards, and association staff and volunteers are available to help guide the college and program director through the process. Where programmatic accreditation is required for employment (e.g., Physical Therapy Assistant), the campus must seek programmatic accreditation prior to program rollout and achieve the grant of accreditation prior to the graduation of the first enrolled class. This requires a huge financial investment and excellent administrative resources from the institution.

Copyright, Fair Use, and Permissions

As educators, we are especially cautioned against violation of the intellectual property (IP) rights of another.

Copyright violations occur when we make unauthorized use of another's work without first acquiring express permission, making proper reference, or insuring we are operating under a fair use exception. "Works" include books, manuscripts, texts, speeches, drawings and other graphics, software, quotations and so on. Intellectual property qualifying for legal protection may be written, spoken, digitized or created in another form.

Because educators are all about books, research, writing and discovery, this is a law that will in intersect with your instructional responsibilities with some frequency.

Your school will have a policy outlining its requirements under the copyright laws. Compliance with the institution's policy will protect both the owner of the intellectual property, your institution, and you in your sourcing and use of teaching materials for the classroom.

The owner of an item of intellectual property has a right in the form of a patent, trademark, or copyright to prevent others from stealing, copying, or taking credit for the property for their own financial or reputational gain. Such rights give exclusive use to the owner for a specified period of time (e.g., may last as long as the owner's life plus 70 years or more for a book!).

When a copyright expires, the work falls into a category called public domain, and is no longer protected under intellectual property law. You can use it freely.

Infringement of copyright law may give rise to civil or criminal charges for the instructor or the educational institution, or both. Infringement among educators typically occurs when quoting, reproducing, distributing, displaying, or otherwise using another's work – such as that of a publisher, consultant, fellow teacher, or a professional associate – to supplement training activities or materials in the classroom, traditional or online.

Limitations and Exceptions

The most frequently used exception to copyright laws in the education space is the concept of "fair use." Fair use allows the use of IP in a face-to-face education setting. This exception is based on the notion of "public good" and allows use of a work without permission. However, note that when using copyrighted property in an educational setting, one must still provide proper attribution to the owner. And, be cautioned, the fair use exception has been deemed not applicable to the for-profit education sector! Most career schools are of the for-profit variety.

Most of the teaching materials in a career school will be authored by the school itself using instructional designers and subject matter experts. This is done in conjunction with a publisher, or by the publisher where the institution pays fees for each student to use the materials. Where the instructor uses institutionally authorized teaching materials, the onus on faculty for copyright infringement related to such materials is essentially relieved.

Where faculty tends to skirt copyright law – and set themselves and the institution up for legal issues -- is by copying and distributing proprietary published materials for use by students where it is not authorized by the syllabus. Sometimes an instructor copies bits and parts of the course text, of ANOTHER text or a library book that is deemed to have useful information, materials from another institution (such as other colleges or training organizations) or intellectual property belonging to an employer or another instructor. Even if you don't get caught, these are violations of copyright law. This practice happens with some frequency – generally because someone wants to do a student a favor, and not out of malicious disregard for the law. Don't do it.

If you wish to use ancillary materials in your course in addition to those standard materials provided, check with your supervisor in advance.

It's safest to stick to the use of authorized course materials. Bottom line, it's never a good idea to use or distribute materials other than approved course materials without express permission of the campus.

Plagiarism

Plagiarism refers to one's passing off another's work as their own. This may involve use of copyrighted material from books or online, or the use of another's non-copyrighted work, such as that of a fellow student. This is obviously not permitted anywhere in an educational institution.

The faculty has responsibility to review papers, exams, and projects for possible acts of plagiarism. And to take action when plagiarism is suspected. Assume the situation will be highly sensitive, thus, it is best to discuss your observations with your department chair, education director or campus president before confronting any suspicious behavior.

Your campus will have a policy, and perhaps a best practice, for responding to suspected cheating. Ask your supervisor for a copy of the Campus Catalog, which is required by accreditors to articulate all academic policies.

It seems the temptation to make unpermitted or unattributed use of another's works is greater in the age of online. Perhaps this is owing to the ease of access, the volume of materials available, the ability to copy and paste, or perhaps ignorance as to the moral and legal ramifications of the practice. To help institutions and instructors with ferreting out plagiarism in works delivered in the traditional classroom or to the online drop box, there are dozens of downloadable software that you can submit suspect material to OR that can run a program against a submitted file. Some of these tools are free for the download. Best to check with your institution as to their best practice and any such product they may advise.

Many institutions make their copyright and plagiarism policies part of every course syllabus. Thus, it is important that as instructors we become educated on these important issues prior to the beginning of class. And to review such policies with students as part of the first night agenda.

Example of a University Academic Integrity Policy

AMERICAN PUBLIC UNIVERSITY SYSTEM

ACADEMIC POLICY ON ACADEMIC DISHONESTY AND PERSONAL INTEGRITY

University Policy

The University System supports and promotes academic honesty and personal integrity. Any form of academic dishonesty has no place in higher education. The University System does not tolerate dishonest efforts by its students. Students who are guilty of academic dishonesty can expect to be penalized. Any student who knowingly assists another student in dishonest behavior is equally responsible. An additional violation of the standards of academic honesty within a course may result in dismissal from the University System.

Plagiarism

The most frequently observed form of academic dishonesty is plagiarism. Plagiarism is the adoption or incorporation of another's ideas without proper attribution of the source. It is more simply defined as taking the writings of another person or people and representing them to be one's own. It is your obligation to read, understand, and comply with the University System's plagiarism policy. If you do not understand this policy, you need to ask your professor for assistance before a plagiarism problem arises. To avoid plagiarism, you must credit the sources used when writing as essay, research paper, or other assignment in accordance with the appropriate style manual or format required in your course. Specific approaches to appropriate citation are found in writing style guides, such as Kate Turabian's *A Manual for Writers of Term Papers, Theses, and Dissertations, 6th Edition or The Publication Manual of the American Psychological Association, 6th Edition.* Types of actions defined as plagiarism: Using a direct quote from a source and not using quotation marks, in-text citation, and reference. Paraphrasing a source and not using in-text citation and reference. Submitting papers, assignments, exams, or forums that were completed by another student, or arranging for another person to complete your assignments for you. Sharing your assignments, exams, or forums with other students. Selling or purchasing (or copying) papers, assignments, or exams from any website that buys or sells them. This also applies if only partially used in student submission. Citing a source with fake bibliographical information. Writing a paper for another student. Submitting a paper, assignment, quiz or exam (or portion thereof) that you submitted in a previous and/or concurrent class without requesting and receiving in writing prior permission from your instructor(s). This also applies to "revising" papers, assignments, quizzes or exams that were previously submitted in any course where credit was received or any course which was previously failed or from which you withdrew, even if it is the same course as your current registration. Copying an image, audio, video, spreadsheet, PowerPoint presentation, etc., without proper citation and reference. Working in a group effort without prior written faculty consent. Consulting source materials or other students without prior written faculty consent. Receiving or giving outside help without prior written faculty consent. Writing a paper in one language and hiring someone to translate it into another language, presenting the translation as your original work. Altering any information on forms or emails after the original has been submitted. Presenting statistics, facts, or ideas that are not your own, or is not common factual knowledge either by the general population, or commonly known within the particular discipline, without citation, even if you view them as common knowledge in your own educational background. When in doubt, cite; definitions or other facts that seem basic to you may still require a citation. For example, the fact that person X is president of a country is a common knowledge fact. Whether that president supports a progressive tax structure or has the majority of electoral support from a conservative base may be known to many but is something that requires citation to support. Using or disseminating materials to third-party websites that buy or sell course work. For information on the consequences of being found plagiarizing, please see the Other Adverse Actions section of the Student Handbook. Plagiarism Detection Turnitin has been integrated into the Assignments tool in all APUS Sakai classrooms.

Summary

Career education is a highly regulated industry. One of the most regulated of industries, akin to Medical and Financial industries. Oversight is provided by States, the Federal Government,

Institutional and Programmatic Accreditors and a myriad of licensing and administrative agencies.

Unfortunately, classroom cheating happens with some frequency in both the traditional college and career education space, so you will want to have read or been trained in your campus policy prior to beginning your teaching responsibilities.

Your understanding and compliance with regulatory requirements is essential to insuring students get all of the services they contracted for, and for making your Campus an excellent Career school!

FACULTY STANDARDS EXCERPTED FROM THE ACCREDITATION MANUAL, 18TH EDITION ACCREDITIING BUREARU OF ALLIED HEALTH SCHOOLS (ABHES)

Copyright © 2010 Accrediting Bureau of Health Education Schools

SECTION E – Program Management and Faculty

Subsection 1 – Program management

V.E.1.a. A program is managed.

Each main and non-main location provides for full-time, on-site oversight for each program which may be met through one or a combination of individuals satisfying the requirements set forth below.

> i. (a) Graduation from an accredited program recognized by the U.S. Secretary of Education or the Council for Higher Education Accreditation (CHEA) in the specialty field or subject area in which they teach (b) Graduation from an otherwise recognized training entity (e.g., hospital-based program) in the specialty field or subject area in which they teach; or (c) Graduation from an institution located outside of the United States and its territories in the specialty field or

subject area in which they teach. The institution must have on file from an agency which attests to the qualitative and quantitative equivalency of the foreign education and the specific courses. The institution must use the credential evaluation services of an agency that has published standards for membership, affiliations to U.S.-based international higher education associations, and are frequently linked to and used by federal agencies, state agencies, educational institutions and employers (e.g., NACES and AICE). Exceptions to this requirement must be justified through documentation of an individual's alternative experience or education in the field (e.g. completed course work, related professional certifications, documentation of expertise).

ii. At least three years' teaching or occupational experience in the subject field.

iii. A baccalaureate degree from an institution accredited by an agency recognized by the U.S. Secretary of Education.

V.E.1.b. The individual(s) responsible for the organization, administration, periodic review, planning, development, evaluation, and general effectiveness of the program has experience in education methodology.

A program provides for management and oversight, including:

i. Recommendation of resources to support the program.

ii. Curriculum development and periodic revision based on learning science and current professional practices in the field of study.

iii. Selection, supervision, assignment and evaluation of faculty.

iv. Periodic assessment and recommendation for modification of facilities and equipment in relation to current professional practices in the field of study.

V.E.1.c. Individual(s) responsible for program management are provided time, resources, and opportunities for professional development.

Professional development activities may include and are not limited to professional association seminars, industry conferences, profession-related meetings and workshops, and research and writing for profession-specific publications.

V.E.1.d. Annual training for individual(s) responsible for program management is provided for the improvement of education-related management skills.

Documentation of training and evidence of attendance is required. Training topics focus on program management functions and administrative responsibilities as it pertains to the educational product.

V.E.1.e. Individual(s) responsible for program management are scheduled non-instructional time to effectively fulfill managerial functions.

Subsection 2 – General faculty requirements

V.E.2.a. Faculty consists of qualified individuals.

Faculty evidence the following:

> i. (a) Graduation from an accredited program recognized by the U.S. Secretary of Education or the Council for Higher Education Accreditation (CHEA) in the specialty field or content area in which they teach; or (b) Graduation from an otherwise recognized training entity (e.g., hospital-based program) in the specialty field or content area in which they teach; or (c) Graduation from an institution located outside of the United States and its territories in the specialty field or subject area in which they teach. The institution must have on file from an agency which attests to the qualitative and quantitative equivalency of the foreign education and the specific courses. The institution must use the credential evaluation services of an agency that has published standards for membership, affiliations to U.S.-based international higher education associations, and are frequently linked to and used by federal agencies, state agencies, educational institutions and employers (e.g., NACES and AICE).

ii. Two (2) years of practical experience in the content area in which they teach.

iii. A current license, certification or other credential if required by local, state and/or federal laws to work in the field, with the exception of those teaching in non-core (e.g., general education) courses.

Individuals who do not meet the above education criteria may qualify through justifying documentation of alternative experience or education in the field (e.g. completed course work, related professional certifications, and documentation of expertise).

These individuals must evidence:

i. A minimum of three years of practical experience in the content area in which they teach.

ii. A current license, certification or other credential if required by local, state and/or federal laws to work in the field, with the exception of those teaching in non-core (e.g., general education) courses. V.E.2.b. Faculty receive training in educational methods, testing, and evaluation and evidence strength in instructional methodology, delivery, and techniques as indicated by evaluation by supervisory personnel within 30 days of beginning instruction, and annually thereafter.

V.E.2.c. Personnel records for all full-time and part-time (including adjunct) faculty meet the requirements of Appendix E, Section B, Records Maintenance, and are up to date and maintained in a well-organized and easily accessible manner.

V.E.2.d. Faculty meetings are held, and the minutes are recorded.

Minutes of these meetings are recorded and include topics discussed, resolution of outstanding issues and record of faculty participation and attendance. The minutes are distributed to program personnel and interested parties in a timely manner.

Subsection 3 – Ratios and teaching load

V.E.3.a. Faculty numbers support program goals, stated educational objectives, and enrollment.

V.E.3.b. Laboratory ratio of students to instructor does not exceed 20 to 1.

A program ensures that the number of students scheduled in a laboratory setting at one time prevents adverse effects on educational delivery. Deviations from the stated ratio are assessed in terms of their effectiveness.

Laboratory numbers may depend on the following factors:

> i. existing professional skills of students
>
> ii. previous educational experience of students
>
> iii. amount of lecture given in laboratory or clinical practice classes
>
> iv. amount of direct supervision provided by an instructor in a laboratory or clinical setting
>
> v. use of technology in providing alternative methods of instruction
>
> vi. type of procedures being demonstrated or conducted (e.g., invasive procedures require greater instructor oversight)

V.E.3.c. Teaching loads for instructors are reasonable at all times.

Allowance is made for non-instructional duties. The teaching load consists of classes taught, contact hours and subject preparation time. Care is taken in assigning administrative duties and classes so as not to overburden faculty.

Subsection 4 – In-service training

V.E.4. Faculty participate in in-service training with a focus on effective teaching at least twice annually.

Documentation of in-service training is required and should include topic(s) discussed, name(s) of presenter, and synopsis of the session(s) presented. Evidence of faculty attendance is maintained in each faculty member's file.

Subsection 5 – Professional development

V.E.5. Faculty is required to participate in professional growth activities annually.

Faculty is provided time, resources, and opportunities for professional development. Documentation needs to demonstrate a combination of professional growth activities which may include, but are not limited to, programs of continuing education, either for professional development or to maintain professional certification, membership and participation in professional organizations, participation in field-related workshops or seminars, and subscription to relevant periodicals or journals. Copies of certificates of attendance, current licensure/certification(s), and any other professional growth documentation are maintained in each faculty member's file.

CHAPTER 5 - HOW STUDENTS LEARN

"Our students are highly motivated adult learners who come to us with lots of life experiences and knowledge. They thrive in a student-centric learning environment in which they are actively involved, theory is applied, skills are practiced until perfected, and feedback on performance is frequent and substantive."

Kathleen Prince, PhD, "Kat", Veteran Educator in the Career Education space, recently retired as Vice President Academic Affairs from ECPI University

Introduction

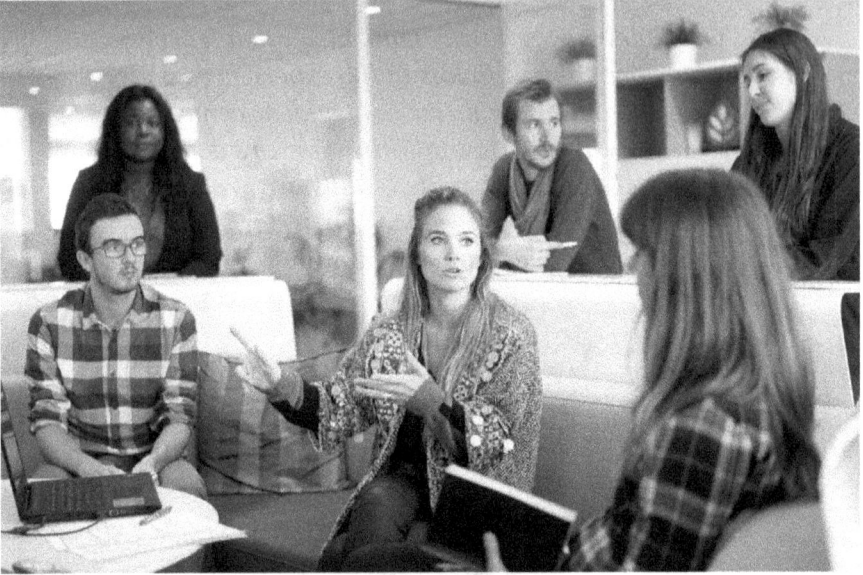

In this section we will assess how students learn and how that advises our teaching. We will discuss the science of learning, the adult learner, and some of the concepts that will come into play in the classroom.

Key Terms

- Active learning
- Adult learning theory
- Andragogy
- Bloom's Taxonomy
- Learning science
- Learning styles
- Pedagogy

Learning Science

Teachers in career education are active, career-changing, or retired Subject Matter Experts (SMEs) in their teaching area. They likely did not study education science in college. Their critical experience comes from training on the job, unlike traditional educators, who often go from high school to college and straight to the classroom. To successfully transition from subject matter expert to educator, the first step is to understand how students learn.

Studies inform us that learning progresses from the simple to the complex. For example, we first learn facts, then concepts, and finally we learn how to synthesize facts and concepts into real life applications. Some students prefer to learn by watching. Others prefer learning by doing. Still others prefer learning by listening, or by combination of all of these different input modalities. Adult students, who come into the classroom with life experience and a more developed sense of self, learn differently than children.

Discussions of learning theories generate questions. Can students actually be taught or is learning more about personal motivation and a supportive environment? What is the instructor's role in learning? Are there other influences on learning? How do you even know if learning has taken place?

So much has been written about it that one can earn a Ph.D. in learning science and even dedicate a lifetime to the study of it. How people learn has been analyzed for nearly two millennia, beginning with Plato and Aristotle. The very earliest philosophers argued whether the brain was a blank slate that drew learning from the environment, or whether knowledge was innate and could be realized through personal experiences and self-reflection. Early Roman thinking emphasized education as a means to develop skills so that citizens could contribute to society, a very practical approach as opposed to the purpose of education being the more abstract search for truth or meaning. Early Roman learning theory is perhaps the genesis of vocational or career education!

Why It Matters

What we understand about how students learn and how we apply these answers to our job as educators is critical to the success of students, ourselves, and the institutions for which we teach. This understanding will guide us in many aspects of our work, such as:

- creating learning objectives
- determining length and components of programs
- establishing the ratio of lecture to practical or hands-on portions of a course
- deciding which subjects are taught first, second, last
- organizing how each topic is presented
- determining the repetition of subjects
- deciding what subjects we can ask students to learn on their own
- deciding how we teach certain subjects
- varying lesson plans and evaluations to address all learning styles or preferences
- reinforcing newly acquired learning

Generally speaking, career schools train students for entry level jobs in medical, technical, business administration, criminal justice, hospitality, transportation, automotive and trades industries. Training includes the requisite technical, hands on skills and also the problem solving, communication and professional behaviors that enable the otherwise proficient technician to get the job done.

By and large, traditional colleges are dedicated to developing students for higher level professional jobs in management, the law, social sciences, teaching and medicine. Traditional schools also focus on liberal arts studies such as art or music, which is usually not a focus of career schools. Traditional schools and educators place less emphasis, if any, on the application of adult learning techniques.

The ultimate goal in career education is to deliver a program in a classroom environment where students can develop defined job skills that are in demand by employers. This work is neither easy nor haphazard. There's a science to creating programs that measure student achievement against learning objectives.

You certainly don't need a Ph.D. to teach in a career school. However, it will help to have a basic foundation in adult learning theory and practice to understand how the programs and courses in your school catalog come about, and why it is so important to follow teaching and evaluation materials provided by your college. Your understanding and application of teaching theories and practices will help you be a better teacher as you see them come to life in your classroom. This in turn will produce more successful and happier students.

> **Andragogy** refers to the study and practice of adult education. The term is derived from the Greek, *andro*, meaning "man", and *agogus*, meaning *leader of*.

Adult Learning Theory

Malcolm Knowles (1913-1997) is one of the foremost authorities on adult learning. Dr. Knowles earned a PhD at Harvard and was a professor in education at such renowned institutions as University of Chicago, Boston University, and North Carolina State University. His entire career was focused on the study of adult learners.

Although not the originator of the term, he introduced the term andragogy to define the study of adult learning in contrast to children's learning. His universally accepted theory of andragogy is characterized by five principles:

1. An adult learner is not entirely dependent on the instructor for learning - Adults are more self-directed.

2. The adult learner's own experience is a resource for learning - Adults will be more interested and learn better when his/her experience is taken into account in the classroom.

3. The adult learner's readiness to learn flows from development of new social or life roles by virtue of growing older.

4. An adult learner's orientation evolves to problem-centeredness - Adults learn by doing. And adults want to apply their learning as soon as possible.

5. An adult learner brings an internal motivation to the learning environment - Adult learners must have their own reason for coming to the classroom.

Children, by contrast, have little or no relevant experience to draw from that they can use to enhance the subject matter or learning. They come to the classroom at an adult's insistence and take all their direction from the teacher. Much of their learning at this stage comes from concrete examples, memorization, mimicking others, and stories.

Pedagogy	Andragogy
Science of teaching children	Science of teaching adults
Learners dependent on teacher for what, why, how	Both teacher and learners actively involved in how to achieve learning objectives and learners can work independently
Little or no prior knowledge on the topic	Learning can be increased by application and adaptation of theory to learner preferences, interests, and experience
Teacher directed and controlled	Learning process elicits relevant learner input to enhance interest, learning, and application
Curriculum oriented	Utilizes learning to problem solve in areas of student interest, work, personal life

The important take away is that adults learn differently. The practices we observed progressing through the grades is not so effective in bringing about student learning and satisfaction in the adult classroom. Most of us grew up in a traditional classroom where the teacher was the authority, or as some say, "the sage on the stage." It is important for instructors in the career education field to change their thinking about program development, course development, instructional delivery, classroom management, testing, etc., so as not to offend and to improve teaching and learning for the adult learner.

Comparison of How Children and Adults Learn

We will review specific examples of effective teaching and learning and classroom management in the adult environment in later sections.

Learning Styles

A popular theory originating in the 1970s is that people have different learning styles. The concept is that when lessons integrate different approaches to teaching that match the array of identified learning styles, students will learn more readily. Walter Burke Barbe's (1926) Learning Styles VAK Model introduced in 1979 breaks down learning styles preferences by visual, auditory and kinesthetic and is one of the more popular inventories. Other theories include seven or more learning styles to include (in addition to Barbe's defined elements) personal, artistic, mathematical, solitary and others.

However, criticism in recent years has been levied at the concept of learning styles. In fact, no empirical evidence has been shown to prove the validity and reliability of learning styles. In effect, no proof exists that students learn better in their preferred style of learning. But we still see the concept being addressed in program development efforts.

At the very least, the delivery of a program in multiple approaches can make learning more interesting and fun.

Depiction of Barbe's Learning Styles Theory

	Approximately one in three people are auditory learners who prefer to learn by listening. This includes listening to speeches, music, audio tapes, etc.
	The largest category of learning preference is visual. Visual learners are great readers, love charts and graphs, and learn by watching demonstrations.
	Kinesthetic learners are just 5% of all learners. They are typically male, hands on, athletic, musical, and like to build and experiment.

In recent years, studies have identified learning styles -- in addition to Barbe's original VAK model – such as musical, artistic, self-directed, mathematical, and more. As an educator, it is important to remember adult learners prefer involvement, variety, and relevance in their lessons. As such, we incorporate a variety of teaching and learning techniques in the program to address personal preferences and to keep lessons active and interesting.

Bloom's Taxonomy

The brain is involved in all aspects of learning, but how does that effect teaching? The brain processes and organizes (stores, connects) outside stimuli, which changes the brain structure over time as it takes in new information. And while human development is defined by specific stages, learning is incremental. Indeed, learning takes place all throughout life.

In 1956 Dr. Benjamin Bloom (1913-1999), an Education Psychologist committed to the study of mastery learning, developed with a committee of educators a model that demonstrates the hierarchical aspect of learning. It is used to organize educational lessons into learning objectives. This model, which came to be known as Bloom's Taxonomy and is considered one of the most significant contributors to learning science, helps educators build increasing levels of learning into courses and programs. This is done through focusing on easier material first, building on facts and concepts, then moving up the taxonomy to practical application and creative use of knowledge. It helps instructors define and students understand the specific boundaries and purpose of a particular course, program, or degree. It also helps define lesson plans and allows for assessment (or measurement) of student learning in each educational setting.

The work of instructional designers, with the help of subject matter expert faculty, is to create a course with learning objectives, lesson plans and learning assessments (quizzes, tests, projects, etc.) that rise through the taxonomy from basic recollection of facts through understanding, application and adapting specified learning to new situations. Identifying the different steps on the hierarchy is done through the selection of verbs and actions to match the various stages. Moving up the taxonomy, a curriculum designer would use the words recall, explain, utilize, justify and so on in order to represent increasingly higher-level learning activity.

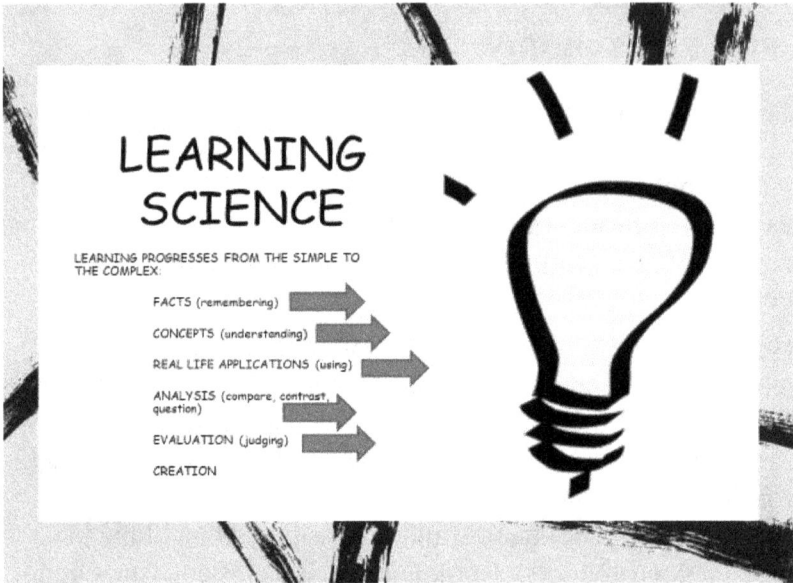

Active Learning

Over 70 years ago, Edgar Dale (1900-1985), a professor at The Ohio State University, created a concept which came to be called the Cone of Learning. The Cone of Learning which demonstrates how active, practical involvement in acquiring new knowledge or skills, contributes to the durability of learning.

As educators we can refer to the graphic representing Dale's theory as an easy way to remember the value of active learning, which is especially so important to adult learners.

Since Dale's initial work, the subject of active learning has been widely studied and accepted as a way to reinforce learning delivered by lecture, and to build mastery of the subject through engagement of students, specifically with each other and in deeper aspects of the subject matter.

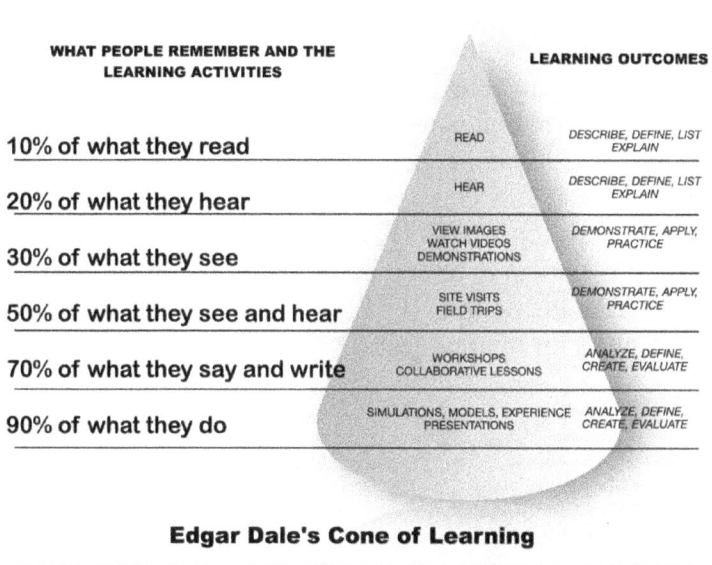

WHAT PEOPLE REMEMBER AND THE LEARNING ACTIVITIES		LEARNING OUTCOMES
10% of what they read	READ	DESCRIBE, DEFINE, LIST EXPLAIN
20% of what they hear	HEAR	DESCRIBE, DEFINE, LIST EXPLAIN
30% of what they see	VIEW IMAGES WATCH VIDEOS DEMONSTRATIONS	DEMONSTRATE, APPLY, PRACTICE
50% of what they see and hear	SITE VISITS FIELD TRIPS	DEMONSTRATE, APPLY, PRACTICE
70% of what they say and write	WORKSHOPS COLLABORATIVE LESSONS	ANALYZE, DEFINE, CREATE, EVALUATE
90% of what they do	SIMULATIONS, MODELS, EXPERIENCE PRESENTATIONS	ANALYZE, DEFINE, CREATE, EVALUATE

Edgar Dale's Cone of Learning

Active learning defines the involvement students in the learning process beyond passive listening. Active learning techniques are almost unlimited starting with the most basic activities of reading, writing, and Q+A. Active learning requires the student to be engaged with the lesson with the five senses, participate in activities that develop higher level thinking and skill development, and reinforces the purpose of the learning objectives. Common examples, beyond the basics, include class discussion, case studies, demonstrations, individual and group projects, field trips, role play, and on and on.

In addition to the opportunity for subject matter mastery, active learning also allows for leadership and collaborative skills to develop, which is also critically important to our work to develop graduates for the workplace.

87

Summary

It is critical to understand that mimicking the educational practices we learned as we progressed through the grades, in high school, and even in traditional college where andragogical models are not as prevalent, is not as effective in bringing about student learning and satisfaction as applying the adult learning model. However, you may have noticed that some elements of adult learning theory and practice were indeed embedded in the traditional K-12 and public postsecondary institutions that you or your children may have experienced. In fact, the concept of active learning is increasingly prevalent in educational models at all levels. Particularly in the adult classroom, it is critical to remember that driving the course exclusively from the podium (i.e., being the "sage on the stage") is just not effective for optimal learning.

CHAPTER 6 – ACTIVE TEACHING AND ENGAGED LEARNING

"Our students come to us from a wide range of places in life. Nontraditional students need nontraditional learning and to be actively engaged in the classroom for learning to be significant. Once the learning becomes relevant, students can start to close the gap from where they're starting to where they want to be. As instructors, it is our responsibility to truly connect with our students to help them cross that bridge. Interpersonal communication is the key to connecting with our students, and these skills modeled in the classroom help students develop and practice those skills which afford them not only academic success and a rewarding career path, but also a positive personal life."

Deborah Robinson, MBA, Communications Studies Faculty, Utah Higher Education System

Introduction

This chapter will convey how the successful teaching and learning of adult students derives from adult learning theory and the best practices of experienced teachers. Teaching adult students will vary from the way you were taught throughout your school years. Adults bring different motivations, expectations, and challenges to the classroom.

Teaching adult students is an acquired skill. And so, to be successful – and to promote and ensure students' success – it is critical to understand what good teaching practice is and to continue to increase your instructional skills throughout your years of teaching.

In career schools, components of hands-on and active learning are most often embedded in the curriculum, including lesson plans and exams, that you will be asked to utilize. Your understanding of how this curriculum comes about and how student performance will be measured against learning objectives is critical to student success. From there, you can incorporate best practice teaching and

> As instructor, your first teaching responsibility is to create a favorable learning climate where every student is engaged and supported in the learning process.

assessment.

Key Terms

- Adult Classroom
- Facilitation
- Theory
- Active Learning
- Hands On/Practicum
- Clinical/Externship
- Course Development
- Learning Objectives
- Assessment

Setting the right tone for the adult classroom

Adult students will better perform and enjoy the learning experience when the lessons in which they participate include the following five elements:

1. The reason the particular subject matter is being taught (how will they use it to solve problems)

2. The relevance of the subject matter to their end goal (e.g., job, career, professional development)

3. Varied lessons and activities to maintain interest and incorporate learner diversity

4. Integration of student prior learning and experience into the course/lesson

5. Understanding that the adult student is not entirely dependent on the instructor for learning

These elements should be addressed with students at the beginning of each course, as well as integrated into the daily lesson plan. In every class meeting the skilled instructor finds a way to relate the learning objectives to the job or industry for which the students are training. When students in the class have a familiarity with the subject matter from previous work experience (for example, a medical assistant transitioning to nursing, a young policeman coming back for his degree so he can be promoted, a massage therapist moving into physical therapy), the instructor should incorporate the students' knowledge and experience into the class with the student's permission and cooperation. Every course should include some independent work such as research or outside interviews where the student is able to learn something relevant to the subject on their own and bring it back to the group.

Because adult students often come to the classroom after having been away from school for a while — and usually with less than outstanding success in prior learning environments they often have the feeling they might not be up to the task. — Thus, instructors in the adult classroom must encourage students that they can be successful, must provide students the options by which to improve, and must explain that instructors and administrators will help them all along the way.

Most of us came up through traditional public or private educational systems where the instructor was considered to be the expert, the source of all knowledge, or as the saying goes "the sage on the stage." While you are the leader in the adult classroom, it is preferable with adult learners to understand your role as a facilitator of learning. It is important at the beginning of each course that the instructor sets the stage for learning in a professional, adult and relaxed context so that students can take on their role as adult learners with responsibility for their own success.

It's always motivating to talk with other instructors about the creative ways they address their course activities while taking into consideration adult learner needs.

Eight best practices for creating an effective classroom climate

Until students understand where the class is going, how you will conduct the class, why the course necessary in their program, and that their dignity will be protected, they will not begin to engage.

Setting the right tone for teaching and learning in the adult classroom:

1. On the first class meeting of every new course, take time at the beginning of the class to introduce yourself by your educational and professional background noting your qualifications to teach the course.

    ☐ Explain a few key points about adult learners and indicate how you will integrate these elements into the course.

    ☐ Review the course objectives and how the knowledge and skills defined in the learning objectives will be relevant to jobs they will be qualified for upon graduation.

    ☐ Explain how the knowledge and skills will be immediately relevant to their lives (can be unrelated to their profession), or ask students to suggest relevance based on their own experience (in their personal lives, in the community, or in their employment)

2. On the first class meeting, ask each student to introduce him/herself on some basic elements AND to answer a question or make a comment related to the course in some way (e.g., what are you most looking forward to, what scares you about this course)

    ☐ Always acknowledge each student's response in some way (e.g., relate their background and interest to your personal experience, thank them for their honesty or enthusiasm, draw comparisons among student responses, etc.).

☐ Take the time you need to hear and acknowledge everyone. This sets a tone of welcoming, respect and teamwork.

☐ As they are talking, take a few notes to remember your students by. How respectful and encouraging it would be for you to refer to this discussion from time to time throughout the course! And this is a great way to learn everyone's name before the end of class.

3. Review the course syllabus in detail on the first meeting. There should be no surprises or areas of confusion about what is coming.

☐ Explain how assessment and grading will work.

☐ Explain academic policies related to attendance, grades, behavior, cheating, and copyright.

☐ At each class meeting, explain the next week's assignments, tests, change in logistics, etc.

☐ At each course meeting, review how the learning objectives and activities for this class relate to the end goal.

4. Provide information on how to get in touch with you to discuss private issues or request academic assistance.

☐ No one expects you to be available 24-7, but some reasonable amount of time for private student interaction must be provided as part of each course meeting or in-between meetings. Your campus may have a policy on this.

☐ This could include office hours, phone calls, emails, meeting before and after class, or time set aside during class for individual meetings which could address both academic and personal issues.

☐ Remember, adult students have full lives and may need an ear and a little input to help them problem solve outside classroom issues, the resolution of which will help them keep or get back on track academically. Careful not to overdo this and become their 'therapist' or BFF.

☐ All campuses have Student Services functions to which you may refer students for additional, more complex assistance, especially for non-academic help such as housing, transportation, finances, daycare, family issues and employment opportunities. Get up to speed on campus resources prior to beginning your teaching assignment.

5. Refrain from sharing too much personal information with a student or the class, especially what is not relevant to the particular subject matter. Sharing professional examples, or personal examples of overcoming adult learner issues, are generally appropriate. This way students learn that there are ways to solve the inevitable problems that will come up. This should be your only reason for sharing personal experiences, never to show off or become involved in students' personal lives.

6. "Check out" in some way with students at the end of every class to identify areas of improvement or follow up.

☐ Ask students "What worked well?" and "What didn't work?"

☐ Briefly summarize today's class against learning objectives.

☐ Explain what is coming next week.

☐ Remind about homework, testing, field trips, etc.

☐ Remind students to see you about academic issues.

7. Always have a review prior to exams, if only to let students know what the exam will cover.

8. Do not test on information not covered in class or assigned for individual study. This can invalidate the assessment experience and is very disheartening for students.

Instructor as facilitator of learning

As an instructor you have optional means of teaching or "getting through to the learner." Learning theory tells us that the adult learner prefers facilitated, learner-centric and practicum learning over an exclusive didactic approach.

Traditional teaching is focused on theory delivered at the lectern. Theory is a didactic approach, involving instructor telling and talking. Almost every course necessarily involves some use of the didactic approach. After all, the instructor has the big picture of where the course has to go to deliver on defined objectives. And the instructor has vastly more experience in the subject matter than the students. And so, it is reasonable and necessary to employ this time worn, instructor-centric methodology in your course. In career schools with adult learners, a good rule of thumb is to keep a lecture to no more than twenty minutes in a given hour, followed by hands-on or group work. In its worst form, over-use of lecture method implies the teacher knows all and is entitled to hold forth exclusively from the lectern.

Facilitated learning is something different than standing in front of the class and lecturing from notes each class meeting. Facilitation is the preferred method of teaching in the adult classroom.

Facilitators are characterized by the following behaviors:

- ☐ Discusses course requirements, learning objectives and administrative details pertaining to the course on the first day of the course, review each week as the course evolves

- ☐ Provides students an understanding of the relevance of all course activities to the job for which their program of study is related

- ☐ Takes input from students about their concerns, fears, questions, experiences, and goals

- ☐ Plans and delivers learning activities that get students engaged, involved, on their feet and provides hands-on experience

- ☐ Minimizes lectures and rote learning in proportion to the overall course (this varies by subject matter of course) and actively engages students in the learning process through both large and small group discussion, case studies, research/papers, lab exercises, games, and so on

- ☐ Provides assessment of learning and evaluation of student progress regularly to each student vis a vis course objectives and assignments

- ☐ Helps students devise action plans to remediate areas of weakness

- ☐ Takes feedback from students as to what's working well and what can be improved

Active learning

The outcome of facilitation is active, engaged learning.

Generally speaking, in career school curriculum, every course will have prescribed components that focus on three areas of instructional delivery – theory or didactic, lab, and practicum (externship or clinical components). While some theory is required in each course to lay out main points and background information, it tends to be the most uninteresting type of learning for most students. Perhaps second only to reading a textbook!

Best practice dictates that once the theory or didactic portion of a course goes beyond twenty minutes, you will lose many students. Minds will wander; students will distract themselves with phones/doodling/talking, and sometimes literally drop out of the class from boredom and frustration.

One very simple way to get students more involved in learning through focused listening to your theory lectures is to ask them to take notes. Even better, provide a very high-level general outline and have them expand the outline with their own notes from your lecture. These make great study tools prior to quizzes and exams. Taking notes engages both mind and body, which reinforces two of the three learning styles.

It is wise to break up theory portions of your lessons throughout a typical four-hour course. This can be done in several ways:

- ☐ Walking away from the podium, moving around the classroom, and asking questions that will summarize your theory points (however, even this is not enough activity or facilitation)

☐ Conducting an oral quiz throughout the lecture or at the end of your lecture on key components – you can let students use their notes!

☐ Breaking into small group discussions to expand on key elements of your lecture (case studies, personal examples, etc.) – ask student groups to report back to the big group on key points they have identified

☐ Showing videos to demonstrate the lecture points and interrupting or following up with questions or breaking into small groups.

☐ Incorporating a combination of these active learning practices is essential. Walking around asking questions after your lecture is the bare minimum.

Another way to add some interest to theory sessions is to pre-assign readings and then to ask students to teach the material either individually or by small group presentation. This can be followed up (reinforced, appended, corrected) by the instructor throughout the discussion or at the end of the class with key points and perhaps a handout. In this way, you are then talking to students who are more invested in the topic.

Almost anything that gets students active in their learning, with parameters defined by and planned out by you, is better than straight lecture! Emphasis is on pre-planning.

Active learning techniques, in contrast with the traditional passive lecture approach, include:

☐ Case Studies

☐ Live Demonstrations by instructor or students

☐ Experiments

☐ Student-made Videos/Multi-media Presentations

☐ Commercial Videos (documentaries, TedTalks, YouTube, cuts of relevant TV shows)

- ☐ Games
- ☐ Crossword and other Puzzles
- ☐ Simulation
- ☐ Vision Boards and Posters
- ☐ Drawing/Building Models
- ☐ Role Playing and Student-led Instruction
- ☐ Group Projects
- ☐ Debates
- ☐ Interviews
- ☐ Online Research and Presentation of Findings
- ☐ Student Reports
- ☐ Field Trips
- ☐ Employer or senior student Classroom Visits

It has been said that the facilitator's role is more about asking the right questions than having answers to all the questions. We would add that wrapping up lessons with the "right answers" (at least according to stated learning objectives and your knowledge as an SME) is a close second in importance.

Today's learning materials from any publisher are generally excellent – extensive, interesting, and contemporary. And so much more effective than textbooks, especially for today's social media-oriented learners. Vast amounts of material are available on the internet or on curated educational websites to support instructors and students in almost every way imaginable. With so much good material available, the instructor's role becomes how best to get this material to students in interesting and impactful ways. You can also satisfy student's need to take responsibility for their own learning by letting them research and bring to the fore any of this kind of ancillary information.

Best practice teaching of adult learners is about creating an interesting, hands-on, relatable, and encouraging environment where students can build on basic theory. Ironically, students who are talking and engaging in the learning process will learn much more than when they are listening exclusively to you sharing your expertise (as great as you are)!

Labs, clinicals, externships

Most courses in career colleges include both laboratory work at the campus to augment theory portions of the program and externship or clinical experience in a live workplace to reinforce technical and professional knowledge and skills learned at the campus. We all remember our college practicum experience, generally with fond memories of how exciting it was to bring our career vision in full focus.

Indeed, accreditors require extern and clinical rotations for specific programs, particularly those in the medical field, specifying hours and types of experiences. These experiences are essential to reinforce practical skills in a real-work environment, and to help students visualize the roles they will play upon graduation and employment. Some experiences are scheduled during the last 1-2 months of the program, and others, such as nursing and higher-end medical programs (surgical technology, respiratory therapy) are interwoven with theory and lab sections throughout the program.

All schools employ Extern and Clinical Staff to secure a sufficient number of appropriate practicum sites for enrolled students, to coordinate logistics and procedures with practicum sites and supervisors, and to assign and check up on students in their practicum portion of the program. This function helps supplement the work of instructors and begins to build the connection between practicum training and going to work upon graduation.

The instructor's role in the practicum portion of the program is to ensure students are taught the necessary technical and professional skills to successfully navigate the experience (and, later, their employment). Hence curriculum is structured to make a clear connection among theory, lab, and practicum portions of the learning. Instructors can be immensely helpful to students and the college in reinforcing students' understanding and visualization of this connection. There is no substitute for the opportunity an externship or clinical rotation provides to build student confidence in their technical and professional skills. High performing students are often invited by the practicum site for full time employment positions once graduated!

Simply stated, performing well in the practicum portion(s) of the program is the gateway to employment upon graduation. It's what they came for.

Lesson plans, learning activities, assessments

The best instructors understand the basics of learning science behind the development of courses, creating learning objective and learning activities, designing quizzes and exams, and selecting support materials for the course. As a career school instructor, you may be asked to create lesson plans for assigned courses. More typically, you will receive standardized materials that you will be required to implement in the classroom. These standardized materials help to ensure compliance with accreditation and industry standards and are most often created with the assistance and guidance of experienced SMEs in your field.

One can obtain a college degree in instructional design, learning technology, or in learning theory and practice. But you don't need a degree to be a successful career school instructor or even to write a good course. In fact, even without an education degree, you may be asked by your campus or accreditor to assist with course development due to your status as a Subject Matter Expert.

Instructional Design (ID)

There is a science to creating to creating courses – it's called Instructional Design (ID) – which focuses on creating student learning experiences that make the acquisition of knowledge and skills more effective, efficient, and appealing. There are various instructional design models; the ADDIE model is the most often referenced example. The ADDIE process, defined below, explains the work of an Instructional Designer (in conjunction with a Subject

Matter Expert) in creating programs and courses for our schools. Virtually every program or course developed follows this model:

- **A**nalysis – Planning the course. Define the learners. What are the objectives of the course? What is the timeline for development? Any constraints (e.g., accreditation requirements, budget, resources, schedule, etc.)? This work is best conducted in cooperation with college academic administration, instructor SMEs, and someone responsible for insuring accreditation standards are incorporated.

- **D**esign – Plan out the course on paper. What content will be covered? In how many units? In what length and in what order? How will the learning be acquired? Define the learning objectives for each unit of instruction in terms of what the student will be asked to know or do. In what delivery modality? Includes Instructor SMEs and College Advisory Board input. Accreditors often provide model curriculum and reviewing other institution's programs is advisable.

- **D**evelopment – Create the content, assignments, assessments, and technology according to the design plan. Instructor SMEs are critical to this phase of development.

- **I**mplementation – Implement the course, determine what works and doesn't, provide feedback to course developer. This is sometimes accomplished through a Beta Test with one or more instructors/classes before rolling out the new course to all students. And generally the Campus Advisory Board of employers/grads will be asked to evaluate the entire course or program prior to rollout, and again after completion of the Beta Test or rollout.

- **E**valuation – How did students perform against the outcomes (learning objectives)? How can the course be better (more efficient, effective and appealing)? Classroom instructors and College Administration should have input at this stage.

Objectives and Learning Outcomes

One of the more difficult tasks of an Instructional Designer is to create student learning objectives (in the Design phase) to effectively support an instructional plan. Learning objectives define what the student is to know or do upon successful completion of the lesson, course, or program.

Learning objectives must very clearly define, through observation and measurability, the desired learner behavior. As such, learning objectives are defined by action verbs. As reviewed in the earlier section on learning theory, objectives progress through the lesson, course and program from basic recollection and statement of facts through application and adaptation to the subject matter.

Practice Exercise:

Which of the following learning objectives meet the requirements of a clear, objective, and measurable learning objective?

> *At the end of the lesson, the student will:*
>
> 1. *Know what a medical emergency is*
>
> 2. *Understand when to administer CPR*
>
> 3. *Articulate the five steps to assess a medical emergency*
>
> 4. *Demonstrate appropriate action for the medical case study at hand*

How Did You Respond?

The first two learning objectives are weak because "know" and "understand" are not observable behaviors. Measuring the student's achievement on these two parameters would be subjective at best.

The next two objectives are better, with the last one being the best. "Articulate", meaning to list or say, is observable and clear. On Bloom's Taxonomy, it is a lower-level activity, for use early in the course or program, because it relies on rote memory to demonstrate the knowledge or skill.

The fourth measure imagines a live case study scenario that requires a learner to actually perform a set of functions against a defined fact pattern. This would require faculty observation of the student who performs application of the knowledge learned (the five steps to assess a medical emergency), to elicit one of the highest levels of achieved learning.

To maximize the learning, a rubric might be used as both a teaching and evaluation tool to define steps and assign a value for each, the total of which add up to a full or perfect score.

Other considerations when writing learning objectives include how many objectives per course or program are appropriate, and how to increase the level of learning throughout the course and the program. As a rule of thumb, one to two objectives per one academic credit hour of instruction is appropriate. There will be multiple sub-objectives for each learning topic. These are issues for review and determination by the ID team.

As for increasing the level of learning throughout the course or program, learning should progress through the lowest level recitation of facts through the application and adaptation of lessons learned throughout the course or program, reflecting the highest level of learning. Some will refer to this as moving up Bloom's Taxonomy. It's helpful to think of a course or a program as a hierarchy of learning. Refer to your school's College Catalog for a listing of courses and definitions which reflect this hierarchy! It will enhance your understanding of instructional design and your school's program plan. It is important for each instructor to review the course syllabi for all the courses in the program you are teaching to observe how the learning is planned and built and the progression through higher levels of learning.

Something to note, repeating the same learning objective in various lessons throughout the course is common and appropriate, even as some objectives will move up the taxonomy. Repetition is a highly effective learning method.

The term learning objectives is interchangeable with the term learning outcomes. Learning outcomes are distinguished, particularly in the world of accreditation, from student outcomes which incorporate learning objectives and those student objectives outside the learning realm – to include student retention/persistence, student

Formative Techniques	Informal Techniques	Summative Techniques	Grading
Ongoing and/or incremental evaluation and/or feedback during the course to give students and teacher a picture of how students are doing	Quick formative assessment with immediate feedback	Formal data driven testing at the end of the course often created by the curriculum design team	Formal summative assessment of student's overall course performance, skills, knowledge

completion/graduation, job placement and student satisfaction.

Assessment

For our purposes, assessment refers to evaluation of student learning, against a given set of learning objectives, through quizzes, tests, papers, projects, presentations, lab exercises, and other means. Assessment is a huge area of ongoing research for educators. It seeks to understand how students learn, whether they are learning, what are they learning, and where are the gaps between objectives and results.

The best kind of assessment is a continuous process that brings results full circle and incorporates findings and recommendations back into the curriculum review, planning and design process. This enhances learning and provides insights and answers to the questions posed above. Here, we will focus on the principles of assessment related to evaluating student performance against defined learning objectives and the resulting student feedback and grades.

Learning is always measured against a set of learning objectives, those defined in the course syllabus. The cumulative assessment of student work results in the student grade for the course.

Remember your own educational background?! Assessment and grading are fraught with student anxiety. Planning for grading so as to reduce student concerns, eliminate subjectivity and comply with course parameters requires instructor understanding and forethought.

Hand in and check off Homework	Q&A, Pop Quiz	Midterm	Incorporates all learning objectives
Lab Exercises	Journaling	Research Paper	Components of final grade and point values known in advance
Student Demo	Feedback from Extern or Internship Site	Class Presentation, Project, Debate	Incorporates Formative & Summative Assessments as defined in course syllabus/objectives
Weekly Test	Class Discussion e.g., What's Working - What's Not	Final Exam or Standardized Test	
Practice Terminology, Games, Crosswords	Small group in-class discussion and/or presentation	Lab Skills Check off	

Assessment of Adult Learners in Career Schools

Career College Best Practices for Assessment and Grading

- As the instructor, you are obligated to ensure students understand exactly what is required to perform at any level (A, B, C, etc.) on each evaluation required in the course – in advance of the test, paper, and performance.

- Grading should be as objective as possible. There should be no subjectivity in the assignment of grades, which dictates that your feelings or relationship with the student is not part of the equation.

- Every assessment should correlate with one or more of the course learning objectives. This helps to ensure the assessment is a valid and reliable indicator of student learning. Testing outside the realm of course objectives, using different words than covered in the course, and introducing new elements not covered in the objectives or the course invalidates the test or evaluation.

- For assignments other than quizzes or exams, students should receive detailed instructions as to evaluation parameters. These include time, length, make-up policy, use of APA or other writing standards, grammar/spelling/punctuation/organization points, appropriate dress for presentations, group behavior/contribution, attribution (credit and copyright), and so forth. Anything that you will include in the grade for the assignment must be explained in advance. I.e., it's all in the syllabus and explained at the first class meeting of every course.

- Incorporating various means of assessment, not just "paper and pencil" quizzes and tests, allows the student to demonstrate higher levels of learning AND provides students with the opportunity to demonstrate competencies in ways that may be more aligned with their learning styles. There are myriad assessment opportunities ranging from research papers and demonstration of skills to projects and role plays and contributions to class discussion.

- The school and your policy for extra credit, do overs, re-takes, make up work/tests should be explained on the syllabus. These are valid learning/assessment techniques so long as they are available to every student. If your organization allows these measures of assessment, you would expect a policy in the School Catalog to outline the parameters related to each measure.

- Many schools include class participation as a grading element to encourage student attendance and engagement. Examples include attendance, positive contributions to the class, assisting other students, and so on. Class participation elements should be explained at the beginning of the course.

- Final grades should be calculated according to the syllabus grading scale, supported by test scores, documentation of class participation, and grades for other assignments. Documentation should be maintained according to school policy, typically requiring faculty use of a grade book and maintenance of test papers and other documentation of assessments for the time period that at a minimum incorporates the timing of the grade challenge policy.

- Instructors must never change a grade to maintain a student's enrollment, to do the student a favor, nor in response to an administrator's request. The only valid reason to change a course grade is for an ERROR made in the calculation of a test or assignment score or in the final course grade OR misinterpretation of a policy.

SUMMARY

Experienced career school faculty will confirm that teaching adult students is very rewarding. You will be so proud of students who move on from your classroom to their practicum and on to their first job in a new career! You will be especially proud of your students who didn't think they could do it.

Your teaching career and students' experience will be much more successful for the understanding you gain from studying adult learners and their special needs. As you move from "sage on the stage" to a facilitator of active learning, your classroom will come alive. There is no end to the ways in which you can engage students in and encourage them to take responsibility for their own learning.

You may be intimated to make first attempts at facilitating active learning. But you must do it in order to become the successful career school educator you want to be. Detailed planning is the key. Try again and again, perfecting techniques as you go.

You will learn new teaching and assessment techniques from the lesson plans that are provided to you, from your fellow instructors, and from engaging in your own professional development and in-service training. And reading about other success stories!

Once you get on your feet as an effective classroom instructor, you are encouraged to participate in curriculum review and development activities, both in your own school and for institutional and programmatic accreditors who typically develop and provide model curriculum for use by member schools. This will enhance your understanding of your students as well as improve your teaching skills, which as a new instructor, is now on your lifelong learning path. And it is always rewarding to meet and share your expertise with others in the field.

Sample Syllabus

Course Title:	Introduction to the Health Care Professions
Course Number:	IHCP100
Course Prerequisite(s):	None
Instructor Name:	TBD
Instructor Contact Information:	TBD
Course Dates:	TBD
Credit Hours:	6.0 quarter credits/ Lecture: 40 hours; Lab: 40 hours)
Course Length:	80 Clock Hours – 20 hours per week/Day 16 Hours per week/Night
Delivery Method:	Blended – Online, Lecture, Lab, Practicum
Required Texts:	*Skills for Today's Medical Professional,* Curriculum Technology
	Keyboarding Practice, Master Keyboarding Software (see Carmen P.)
	Medical Dictionary, Merriam-Webster's

ISBN 0877798532

Other Reference Materials:	First Aid Guide and Materials
Course Description:	This introductory module provides the foundational information and skills that students will utilize throughout their chosen healthcare program of study. The course provides an overview of the healthcare professions, including the history of medicine, ethical standards, medical terminology, and behaviors that are expected of professionals in the field. Strengthening student skills in writing, basic math, and keyboarding is a focus of the course. Personal development topics such as financial management including an overview of credit, and professional networking skills are also addressed.
Objectives:	By course completion, students should be able to:
1.	Discuss the history of medicine
2.	Explain and apply medical ethics and their application to workers in the healthcare industry including HIPPA
3.	Describe the various word parts and their meaning in medical terminology and utilize medical terminology accurately
4.	Take and record vital signs accurately
5.	Perform Basic First Aid
6.	Discuss the value of networking and volunteering in building a foundation for career success
7.	Demonstrate the appropriate habits,

	attitudes, and behaviors for the professional environment
8.	Discuss the responsibilities, benefits and risks involved with personal loans and other types of borrowing
9.	Develop a personal monthly budget plan
10.	Describe and apply the basic units of measurement commonly utilized in the healthcare industry
11.	Demonstrate compliance with the standards of effective interpersonal, telephonic and written communications in a professional environment

Teaching Strategies:	This course is presented in lecture and practicum formats with the use of learning exercises, group discussions, computer-based learning, case studies, homework, and related activities.

Evaluation Methods:	**Point Values:**
Homework and Lab Assignments	30%
Quizzes	25%
Keyboarding	10%
Participation*	10%
Final Exam	25%
Total	**100%**

*Participation includes attendance, productive participation in discussions, and active engagement in the lecture/learning activities.

Course Completion Requirements: Students must achieve a passing grade and submit all required exercises and projects, complete all required quizzes and examinations, and meet the standards of the school attendance policy.

Make Up Work Policy: Students are required to make up all assignments and work missed. The instructor may assign additional outside make-up work to be completed for each absence. Arrangements to take tests and/or quizzes missed because of an absence or tardy can only be made with the instructor's approval. Hours conducting make-up work cannot be accepted as hours of class attendance.

Classroom Policies:

- To maintain satisfactory attendance, students will be warned and counseled if they are absent more than 20% of a course. Students who have been absent for 10 consecutive scheduled class days will be dropped from the training program. If students are absent for 50% or more of a module, they will be notified that they have failed the current course and may be placed on academic probation. Students will be required to repeat the course.

- Students who are required to participate in military duties and are absent from their scheduled classes will not be penalized. Students must provide the College with written documentation verifying the required military leave and length of time requested.

- Students are required to wear the designated college uniform during training. Students are expected to dress professionally during class time, including during their work in practicum sites.

- A student who acts in an unethical or unprofessional manner on a test or an assignment will receive a grade of "0" for that test or assignment. A second incident of unethical or unprofessional behavior may result in administrative termination from the college.

- Use of cell phones in the classroom during class time is not allowed; and, if they are used or ring during class, the faculty member may confiscate them for the remainder of the class and report the behavior to the Program Director/Director of Education.

- Behavior that persistently or grossly interferes with classroom activities is considered disruptive and may be subject to disciplinary action. Such behavior inhibits other students' ability to learn and instructors' ability to teach. A student responsible for disruptive behavior may be required to leave class pending discussion and resolution of the problem and may be reported to the Program Director/Director of Education.

Academic Dishonesty: All student work is to be submitted to faculty and represent the student's original work. If other sources are used as references, each source must be identified. Plagiarism and falsification of documents, including documents submitted to the College for other than academic work, will be addressed in conjunction with Campus academic policy and may result in disciplinary action.

Course Outline Calendar: Note: The syllabus will provide a high-level weekly outline for students which denotes the distribution of lecture, lab, keyboarding, and other learning modes. The course outline also includes reading and homework assignments as well as quiz and test dates.

Instructors are provided more detailed corresponding course outlines (e.g., daily) to guide their presentation of the class in conjunction with all course requirements.

The instructor should review the syllabus, including the high-level daily outline, with students on the first day of class (repeating each Monday as new students are integrated into the course).

More detailed information must be reviewed with students on a daily basis to ensure they understand both in-class and outside-class requirements.

Course Outline

The syllabus will provide a high-level weekly outline for students which denotes the distribution of lecture, lab, keyboarding, and other learning modes. The course outline also includes reading and homework assignments as well as quiz and test dates.

Instructors are provided more detailed corresponding course outlines (e.g., daily) to guide their presentation of the class in conjunction with all course requirements.

The instructor should review the syllabus, including the high-level daily outline, with students on the first day of class (repeating each Monday as new students are integrated into the course). More detailed information must be reviewed with students on a daily basis to ensure they understand both in-class and outside-class requirements.

Course can be started in any week. Each Monday includes an Introduction component for new students that will include content such as appears in the following example:

DAY 1

College Skills	Campus visits	Medical Skills	Lab Activity	Homework	Outside hours
Interpersonal communications	Library tour	Medical terminology, A+P, Muscular system	Keyboarding	Chapter 1 of the textbook	One hour

CHAPTER 7 – CLASSROOM MANAGEMENT

"Classroom Management should not be about managing the classroom. It should be about creating a safe, nurturing and engaging collaborative environment where all students feel secure enough to open their minds and immerse themselves in the learning experience. That is not an easy task for many who enroll in our schools. However, in an environment like this, students will come to know the instructor as a leader, coach, and trusted guide on a life-changing academic journey."

Graham Nott, MA Learning Technologies, Vice President Academic Affairs, Concorde Career Colleges

Introduction

Adult students can be challenging. This chapter will introduce classroom and student scenarios that you may be exposed to in the exercise of your teaching responsibilities. We will review classroom management principles and best practices, the issues that impact student-instructor relations, and institutional ramifications such as regulatory compliance and legal liability.

Two key takeaways:

- Student behaviors will challenge your interpersonal skills and problem solving abilities. As a new instructor, your expectation may be that adult students will be focused, polite, in control of their emotions, willing to listen and able to learn, professional, appreciative of your help and experience, and so on. However, many students feel insecure about their academic abilities and may not yet have developed the requisite interpersonal skills to resolve the problems and conflicts that arise in a professional environment. These dynamics raise the stakes of almost all instructor/student interactions.

- The educational institution will be held accountable for its instructors' behaviors. Instructor interactions with students may lead to legal, regulatory, and public relations issues for the institution. As such, instructors are obligated to be familiar with and committed to best practices for the resolution of student conflicts.

Key Terms

- Classroom Management
- Rules of Engagement
- Proactive
- Professionalism
- Best Practices

Principles and Practices for Managing the Adult Classroom

With regard to instructor-student interactions, as you gain experience you will discover what works and what might make matters worse! Based on adult learning theory and the experiences of educators who have gone before you, following is a compilation of best practices for effectively managing the classroom beyond delivering curriculum:

1. The instructor is responsible for managing the learning environment, setting a tone that allows all learners to be comfortable and supported. This is not a one-time conversation. Success requires ample preparation, effective communication and continuing oversight.

2. Successful instructors are proactive and review with students the rules of engagement on the first meeting of every new class. Advise them to expect you will address negative behaviors (e.g., fighting and bullying, absences/tardies, cheating, and lack of participation) which, if unresolved, will have an impact on the student's grade or result in dismissal from the class. Familiarize yourself with student policies articulated in the Campus Catalog prior to conducting the introductory meeting of your class. Be advised by the DOE or Program Director in advance of your

class about policies such as cell phone usage in the classroom, internet practices, consequences for absences and cheating, and other important policies that will inevitably come up in your classroom. Review these policies with your students the first night of class.

3. You might consider repeating some of the rules prior to giving a test, when breaking students into work groups, or when multiple examples of unprofessionalism have occurred. To set the proper learning and professional tone prior to the beginning of each class, develop a ritual such as asking a question that effectively allows you to "check in" with each student and determine any festering issues prior to the start of class. Be sure to manage the time such as allowing each student to speak for one minute. This does not have to be related to the lesson. Examples:

    *   If you could be anyone else but yourself who would that be?

    *   What was the best thing that happened to you since the last class meeting?

    *   From whom do you hope your next cell phone call or text to be?"

    Make it fun or thought-provoking and useful in determining the mood of the class. It may be relevant and useful to link responses to the "rules of the road" or this class lesson in some way.

4. A universal leadership principle is to "praise in public and admonish in private." Individual behavioral and academic issues should always be addressed in private, never in front of the class nor in earshot of other students.

5. A critical element of the student's academic and professional development is the acquisition and practice of effective workplace skills to include self-awareness, emotional self-control, problem solving, compromise and professional decorum. This theme should thread through every course and delivery modality (lecture, lab, online, individual and group work). This should be talked about at the beginning of the class, and as often as necessary thereafter, to help justify your classroom management principles and practices.

6. Review student behavioral issues as they occur with your Program Chair or the Director of Education. Especially if you are unsure about how to resolve the situation, if earlier interventions have not worked, and if you sense students are unhappy about your intervention.

7. When working with students to resolve issues, address specific observed behaviors and their consequences (aligning with your stated rules of engagement) rather than student's personalities, perceived motivations, deficiencies, etc. For example, it creates less defensiveness to reference the arguing, eye rolling, class discomfort, and lack of compliance with professional standards and the effect they are having on the learning environment rather than sharing your perception of student's motivation (e.g., lazy, lack of commitment) or personality (e.g., immature, angry, rude).

8. It will be difficult or impossible for an instructor to maintain requisite classroom decorum with individual students after having crossed the line of professionalism.

   It's never okay for an instructor to engage with students in the following ways:

   - friend/communicate with students on any form of social media
   - meet students for lunch, coffee or drinks
   - ride-share or carpool with students
   - date, flirt or engage in personal relationships with students
   - loan or give money to students
   - provide/receive personal services (e.g., babysitting, personal shopping)
   - sell or buy goods (e.g., Girl Scout Cookies, Oils)
   - exchange money or food stamps
   - collect for or contribute to each other's charities
   - share personal or confidential information about other students

- promote your own religious, political, or social/cultural opinions

- share personal information unrelated to course objectives

- meet outside the classroom except for: Fieldtrips, Community/Volunteer events pre-approved by the campus, at Extern sites only when student supervision is part of your job

- engage in activities of a personal nature (if you have to wonder, it's probably not okay)

9. In the course of your employment, you may experience differences with your Program Director or other members of the campus leadership team. You may think that you are not paid enough. Your opinion of school policies or procedures may not align with management. The lab may not be set up in the way you like. You may think the Admissions Team is too aggressive. These are legitimate issues to take up with your Program Director, Director of Education, or the Campus President. These are never topics for discussion with students in or outside the classroom. Period.

10. There will be a wide variety of talent and motivation among students in most of your classes. This is normal. Outcomes will array along the bell curve especially the larger the group and over time. Sometimes a whole class seems not to be "getting it." This is not normal. This is on you! Perhaps exam questions do not reflect the course objectives detailed on the syllabus. Perhaps subjects tested on were not covered or were glossed over too quickly. Some subjects are more difficult than others. Sometimes students in the beginning of their program haven't yet gotten the hang of how to learn, take notes, ask for help, or study. These are normal especially when you begin teaching or when students are new to their program. When this happens, you must take responsibility. Dig deep for the answer(s), use the exam as a teaching tool, be prepared to re-administer an exam, and ask your supervisor for help. It's hard to imagine a situation that is the students' fault when the whole class fails. It's the instructor's job to make every reasonable effort to bring all students along, not weed the weak ones out.

11. Being ultra-prepared for every class helps eliminate appearing unprofessional, making mistakes, getting off topic, running out of time and student dissatisfaction with the course. Arriving at least a few minutes before class will allow you to appear ready for and enthusiastic about today's class, and help you pick up on extra-curricular concerns that may be going on. Detailed preparation for labs and practicum exercises (e.g., breaking into small groups for discussions) is essential to keeping students safe, ensuring all students are participating and achieving course objectives. As discussed in the introduction, it takes time to learn how to best deliver a lesson, how long things take, where the roadblocks are. There is no substitute for detailed planning. You will improve!

12. Postsecondary education has become a highly politically-charged topic in recent years. Politicians and the public discuss everything from student debt load to loan rates to the rising cost of tuition to lack of student preparedness to graduation rates to availability of jobs for college grads, and so on. These are indeed important and interesting topics for those of us who work in higher education. As you gain experience as a classroom instructor you will certainly develop knowledgeable opinions on these subjects. Indeed, you should be encouraged to learn as much as you can about these topics and to develop an informed opinion. However, these complex and polarizing topics are not recommended for discussion with students. Such discussions may leave students feeling discouraged about their academic and career choices.

Impact of Classroom Management Issues on Campus

Your employer could be negatively impacted in small or large measure by ineffective or improper handling of classroom issues. This could encompass student or parent lawsuits, negative Better Business Bureau and YELP reviews, poor student extern and employer site relations, punitive actions by the State or U.S. Department of Education, and Accreditor citations or sanctions.

Even general dissatisfaction leading to poor survey ratings among your students can be costly to the institution.

In the conduct of your course and related administrative tasks, you represent your employer and your campus. Should any situation you direct or participate in rise to a serious level, your employer will inevitably be held accountable by students, regulators and other stakeholders. Through the documentation and enforcement of policy, the campus attempts to assist faculty in creating the best possible learning environment for all students, and to insure compliance with all campus objectives and regulatory requirements. An instructor's knowingly or negligently creating issues for the campus is grounds for disciplinary action and perhaps termination.

Hot Button Issues

Areas of particular concern for instructors – i.e., those that can lead to student dissatisfaction, regulatory non-compliance and poor public relations -- include attendance taking, assignment of grades, changing of grades and attendance, delivering the requisite number of class hours, not teaching to the objectives, checking-off practical skills, student bullying and fighting, gossiping about competitors and other stakeholders, adhering to ethical standards of practice, internet and social media practices, and fraternizing with students. Your campus will have a faculty handbook or instructor training which will cover faculty expectations in these areas.

SUMMARY

Preparation for both Academic and Classroom Management aspects of the instructor role prior to stepping into the classroom is essential! Be proactive!

Schools are required by their States and Accreditors to maintain Student Services such as financial counseling, retention management, job placement and referral to social service and law enforcement agencies to address student extracurricular needs. For issues beyond classroom-related concerns, instructors should refer students to the Student Services Office for assistance. In such cases, the instructor should let the student know that a referral will be made and advise the Student Services office so that an employee can be proactive in reaching out.

Instructors should never share any personal concerns about the industry, the school, campus employees or other highly charged educational issues with students. Neither faculty nor students are prepared to adequately assess the complexity of these topics and their impact on your assigned students. As an instructor, you may be tempted to gripe about wages, gossip about the Program Director's new haircut, wax about politics or financial aid, and so on. This can infuse students with doubts and fears about their decision to pursue a professional education, and most certainly models unprofessionalism. Should students express concerns about the school or the industry, a referral and "heads up" to the Program Director or DOE is in order.

Problems in the classroom are inevitable. Defining professional requirements at the first class and addressing issues as they arise is the best practice for achieving a successful classroom experience for all. As for yourself, just like your students, commit to practicing professionalism every day!

Case Studies for the Application of Best Practice Classroom Management Principles

The following scenarios are typical of encounters you will have with students in the exercise of your teaching responsibilities. Using the best practice principles discussed in the first part of this chapter, determine the steps you would take to best resolve the issues you identify.

Situation #1:

Two students in your morning class don't like each other. When one of them answers in class, the other rolls her eyes or makes a critical remark. One refuses to participate in group projects with the other. Their interactions before and after class are loud and heated. Other classmates are taking sides, while others seem bothered by the disturbances. You tried ignoring them, it hasn't stopped.

Situation#2

A student indicates she would be willing to buy groceries for you with food stamps in exchange for cash. "You can make a list of stuff you normally buy; I'll pick it up and bring it to your car before class. You could pay me 75 cents on the dollar."

Situation #3

Students just finished their medical terminology final exam and are headed to Bahama Mama's to celebrate. And it's Roxanne's birthday. They ask you to join them.

Situation #4

You receive regular requests from students to be friends on Facebook and to follow you on Instagram. You have an active Twitter account where you wail on the folly of internet dating sites.

Situation #5

The lab supplies your supervisor promised to order for your Pharmacy Tech class have not arrived in time for you to conduct today's lab. You are fuming...

Situation #6

Almost every day a student or two sits in the back of class texting and surfing the web. They don't participate in class discussions, and when assigned to small groups to conduct assignments, they remain distracted by their phones. Their assignments are often late, their test grades are not so great.

Situation #7

You think you may have seen James cheat on the Evidence exam. You say nothing. When you review his test, his answers are perfect. In fact, his answers match all of William's answers (whom he sits next to). This is the third exam of the course, he earned C grades on the last two tests and he's missed three out of 10 class meetings this term.

Situation #8

You are perturbed that one of your students texted you on a Saturday evening to inquire about an assignment in your online Coding course. You feel that the weekend is your time, and that this student is being rude to disrupt your peace and quiet.

Situation #9

One of your former solidly performing students has come to you to complain that he is not being helped by the Placement Office to find a suitable externship site. If the student fails to start his practicum in one week, he will be dropped for excessive absences.

Situation #10

Your Massage Therapy students are having difficulty with the draping technique. You agree to model the technique and strip to your underwear, lie on a table, and direct the students to watch as your best student demonstrates the technique.

Situation #11

One of your second term Respiratory Therapy students is not performing well in the class, and you are concerned about her safety with patients once she goes to a clinical site next term. The student often debates your input, doesn't do well on exams, hasn't passed the skills check off, may have a receptive language deficiency, and indicates she intends to report you to administration for being prejudiced against her ethnicity.

Situation #12

There are rumors that a nearby career school is about to close. You've read that the U.S. Department of Education conducted and audit and has fined the school for irregularities in its Financial Aid practices. A couple of students made a few cracks about this in class today. One concerned student approached you after class and asked if you knew anything about the rumors, and whether you were confident in your campus' financial aid dealings. The student said he was concerned about his own financial aid account with the school because he provided "doctored up" tax returns to the Financial Aid office when he was admitted.

Situation #13

None of your nursing students did well on the Pharmacology Exam. You plan to sternly lecture them at the beginning of the next class about their lack of motivation and potential to fail the nursing program and the NCLEX.

Situation #14

One of your nursing students is wearing red nail polish and hoop earrings. This just makes your blood boil. In your day, nursing students were not allowed to dress as hussies.

Situation #15

A student breaks a thermometer in the lab during a practicum session on taking vitals. You know about mercury contamination, but you allow the class to finish their exercises on the check-off list because it's the last day of lab.

CHAPTER 8 – DISTANCE LEARNING

"It is a common misconception that distance education and online learning creates a sense of separateness or disconnect between faculty, students and the curriculum. Quite the contrary, a thoughtful approach to online delivery provides those immersed in distance education more poignant and planful opportunities to engage with one another and the subject matter. Moreover, at the heart of online learning lives the promise of expanded access and a quality higher education, regardless of location or circumstance."

Amanda Lynn Smith, PhD, Curriculum and Instruction, Senior Vice President, Academic Services and Products, Academic Partnerships

Introduction

Distance or Online Learning has been one of the most important and impactful trends in higher education. It's been nearly a generation now since the delivery of education, in the context of the instructor and student being separated in space and time, took a serious hold. As such, Distance Learning deserves its own chapter.

This chapter will introduce you to distance learning concepts, terminology and findings over the past decade. It is not intended to teach you how to teach online.

The term Distance Learning is interchangeable with Online Learning, Online Education, Distance Education and e-Learning. Distance Education has its roots in Correspondence Schools, popularized in the early 20th century as a means to educate people without access to universities to learn a skill. Correspondence Schools distributed books, lessons and tests to students by mail; students completed their lessons and returned them to the school for a grade. Today's distance education is characterized by its use of technology to deliver content and to facilitate student to student and instructor to student communication and interaction.

Distance Education has been around for a generation; we've learned a lot and teaching and learning is improving all the time. The 2020 world pandemic has given rise to application of distance learning to student populations beyond the postsecondary market, to new delivery platforms, and to expanding conversations about the pros and cons of distance education.

One seemingly un-debatable notion today is that distance education is certainly here to stay.

KEY TERMS

- Asynchronous
- Engagement
- High Touch
- Platform

Distance Learning – WHAT IS IT?

It's Asynchronous

The fundamental idea of distance learning is that, in the delivery of the course, the teacher and student are separated in location and time. This characteristic is referred to as asynchronous. The purpose of the asynchronous relationship between students and faculty is to give students more access when they are otherwise located too far from a campus to fulfill attendance requirements, when campus logistics (course calendar, begin and end times) do not accommodate a student's employment schedule or other commitments, or when the student wishes to enroll in a program or a course that is not available at the campus (e.g., does not offer a nursing program, only offers associates degree). Also, some campuses offer a course in an asynchronous format to provide access to a specific instructor expert to whom students would not otherwise have access. And sometimes, students simply prefer distance learning over traditional college classroom learning for their own reasons.

Depending on the institution, students can take an entire program of study by distance (e.g., Western Governor's University, University of Phoenix) or just a course (e.g., many career colleges offer their General Education courses only through distance).

Where student and instructor engage online at the same time or, alternatively, not online but at a physical distance with some materials being distributed through the web (e.g., email or posted on the campus website) is sometimes referred to as distance education. But these practices are more accurately described as remote learning or delivery. This method was characteristic of schools transitioning out of the traditional classroom during the 2020 global pandemic. This text does not address remote learning, a term that you are hearing more and more in the press.

It Replicates the Traditional On-Ground Experience

Just as in an independent study, an online course seeks to replicate the traditionally delivered on ground course online. Educators are obliged to essentially replicate online the traditional on-ground version of course. This means that assignments, assessments, attendance, submission of completed assignments, classroom discussions and other student performances -- and even student services -- must be translated through learning activities, assessment practices, operational procedures and so forth to provide an equivalent student experience in pursuit of the same course objectives as the traditional course.

Over thirty years ago when technology began to pervade our everyday lives, there was a popular saying, "If you're going to be high tech, you have to be high touch." This seems so relevant in the world of distance education. In distance education this means that the user, in this case the student, needs to feel at ease in interacting with the course delivery platform, in understanding and fulfilling all requirements of the course, and in accessing all the academic and administrative services provided by the campus. This means easy to sign in, easy to read, easy to follow instructions, easily accessible add-ins, less clicks, fast downloads, and perhaps most importantly the student can get help in a reasonable amount of time to resolve issues and stay on task. Not to mention effective access to faculty and administration. All while participating in a course of at least the same level of content, difficulty and learning as the traditionally-delivered course.

It's All About Student Engagement

Student engagement -- with the course and the learning activities, with other students, and with the instructor – is a particular focus for the Instructional Design Team including SMEs and Technical advisors to the team. Without the advantages of face to face encounters in the traditional classroom, the instructor and students need lots of opportunities and tools to make sure communications all around are interpreted accurately.

Without ongoing effective student engagement in the course, with other students and faculty, and with campus administration for extracurricular concerns, students have proven to become discouraged, drop out and fail the course.

Embedding and effecting high touch and high engagement in online coursework so as to replicate on ground communications, teaching, learning and assessment is no easy task. Not for the Instructional Design team. Not for instructors. Not for College Administrators.

Distance Learning – WHY IS IT?

Distance Education came about in response to students who wanted a college education, but who had limited access to a university. Limited access comes about for some potential students due to geographical distance between the would-be student and the institution, as well as the would-be student not being available during traditional university hours (work, family obligations).

Online Education was initiated in the late 1980s by Dr. John Sperling, founder of University of Phoenix (UOP), in response to police officers whose work schedules didn't permit them to attend classes and get their degrees in the traditional setting. With only five traditional campuses left, UOP's student body has almost completely transitioned to online.

Furthering its appeal, distance courses can be readily available for the taking. Some courses are only offered in the traditional setting in certain terms, and sometimes only once a year.

And some modern students who grew up online and with technology are just more comfortable completing their education in an online format. It has become a matter of personal preference.

For today's workers, many who travel on a regular basis, getting a college education can be impossible by traditional means. With Distance Education, however, one can be a student anywhere anytime. Many working students juggle work and school more effectively through non-traditional online delivery.

As online programs have grown in popularity among students for the reasons stated, employer acceptance of the validity of an online degree has come along also. There's a growing recognition that there are additional benefits to getting a degree online, including learning how to effectively utilize technology, improving communication skills through remote means, accomplishing work tasks in an online environment, and improved focus and time management that comes with distance learning.

Growth in online programs among both undergraduate and graduate programs has been steady through the last twenty years. Following is a snapshot of the growth from 2012-2016 (the latest graph available). 2018 USDOE statistics indicate one third of all college students take at least one course online.

STUDENTS TAKING DISTANCE COURSES BY LEVEL - 2012-2016

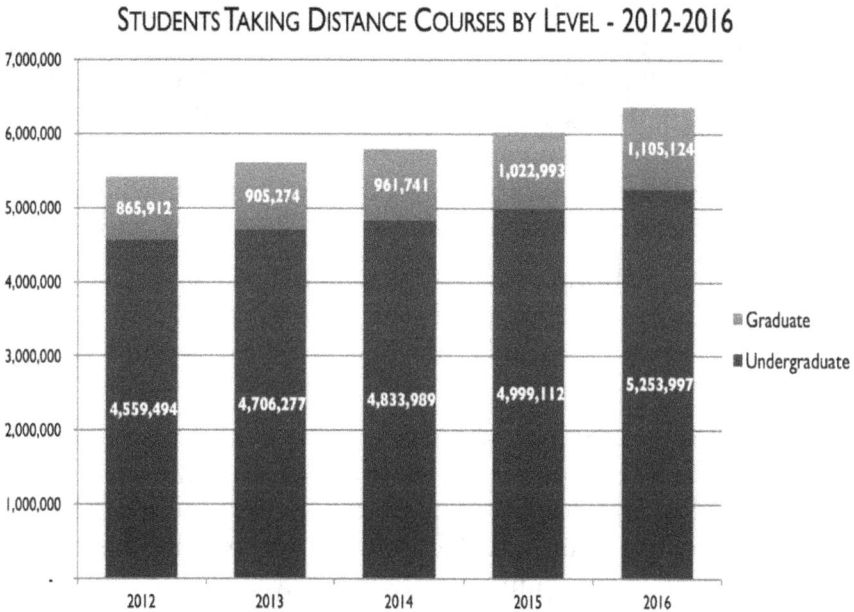

Graph data, Undergraduate and Graduate:
- 2012: 4,559,494 / 865,912
- 2013: 4,706,277 / 905,274
- 2014: 4,833,989 / 961,741
- 2015: 4,999,112 / 1,022,993
- 2016: 5,253,997 / 1,105,124

Nearly 7 million or 1/3 of postsecondary students enrolled in online education in fall 2018 – including whole programs or one course

USDOE *National Center for Education Statistics*

Ten Essentials of an Online Course

Educators have come a long way towards integration of high touch and high engagement in distance delivered courses over the past twenty years. Developing online courses follows a similar path as the traditionally delivered course. Because of the distance aspect of online learning, the Instructional Design Team professionals redouble their efforts to create active, engaging learning experiences. And, as you might imagine, the technical aspects of the delivery platform -- to support students, faculty and administrators' needs in teaching, learning, customer service, academic record keeping and regulatory compliance – are a significant and critical focus.

133

1. Every distance course lives on an electronic platform which houses the substantive teaching-learning elements, i.e., the course and the essentials of campus administration. To guide learners, platforms are organized similarly to other web applications with a menu, icons, pictures, instructions and links. Online platforms have become highly intuitive but may take students a few sessions to gain familiarity and comfort.

2. The online platform provides the required course elements such as course syllabus, the instructor's name and contact information, quizzes and exams, assignments, learning activities.

3. The online platform provides academic and administrative support such as grade cards, counselling, academic warnings, notice of policy and procedures, and campus announcements. The learning platform doubles as the classroom and the gateway to campus administrative services.

4. The campus must provide extracurricular support through online communications and documents, telephone calls or email, in person meetings where feasible – this may come through the platform, phone, mail or email, in person meetings or all of these.

5. The online campus must translate attendance taking, typically completed each class meeting in the traditional classroom. Because online delivery allows students the flexibility of completing weekly course requirements at their own pace, attendance is typically reflected once weekly when a student submits an assignment to the drop box by a certain deadline. Assignments required to be posted to the drop box by certain dates/times also ensure students are making regular progress on course objectives throughout the course rather than "telescoping" a course all in the last week of a course.

6. The lecture portion of an online course is provided in short, impactful segments. These may be provided on Power Point slides, in narrative format, or by course instructor video. Lectures are enhanced with charts, photographs and illustrations, summarization of key points in boxes, video clips, and so on. As with traditional delivery, these lectures typically coordinate with the course textbook and/or other reading materials made available to students. Readings with ample reinforcement of lessons through assignments, practice exercises and other activities that support an array of learning styles keeps students engaged and help insure learning. Readings are sometimes online, and sometimes a traditional textbook is used to support the course. Some publishers provide an electronic textbook in lieu of a paper version.

7. Required assessment is made through instructor's evaluation of student performance on quizzes and exams, papers submitted to a drop box, evaluation of contributions to student group discussions or projects, and more.

8. Instructors are responsible to interact regularly and effectively with online students throughout the course. This happens privately on the course platform, through email, in group discussions, and through phone or face to face meetings where feasible. Instructors are required to provide "office hours" so that students can easily connect as needed. Because the instructor is not on the podium in an online course, the range of contact hours must reflect availability to students in various time zones and on weekend and evenings when adult students are typically completing classes online.

9. A typical way to make online learning more high touch is through the use of student to student and/or faculty to student chat rooms or discussion boards. This helps students not to feel isolated and can provide a ready check on learning and provide enhanced learning through exposure to various opinions flowing from student's diverse locations and experiences. Students may be evaluated on their contributions to discussions, from both quantitative and qualitative perspectives. This requires the instructor's explanation or a grading rubric to be included with the course syllabus to ensure students know how contributions will be evaluated.

10. Students must have access to adequate and reliable technology - including hardware, software and connectivity - to effectively participate in online education programs. Students have proven to be creative in equipping themselves for the task through public Wi-Fi, the use of library resources and even through their smart phones. Typically, students have been more eager and better prepared to participate in distance education initiatives than their instructors.

Faculty Onboarding

We spent time in previous chapters explaining the necessity of transitioning the mindset from traditional delivery of education to facilitated, active learning methodologies to better support adult learners. Similarly, teaching online will require training and transformation. It's like learning to play poker online – it's the same game, rules and scoring, but the platform and the distance takes some getting used to.

Your campus will require you to participate in distance education onboarding activities if you are going to teach an online course. The course will review your role and responsibilities, the technology, policies for academic compliance and student support, operational procedures and regulatory requirements. And you will learn to navigate the platform. Perhaps you'll be assigned a mentor until you are fully up to speed.

Like anything new, online teaching will probably feel clumsy and may have its frustrations at first, but instructors get used to it quickly when they are open to learning something new.

What We Know Now

Early on, some online education proponents believed distance education would be a way to save on the cost of education delivery through increasing class sizes, expanding student to instructor ratios, reducing real estate costs, and lowering numbers of administrative staff.

On the other hand, some worried that asynchronous aspects would cause student retention and completion to suffer significantly and soon bring the new methodology to a halt.

A number of truisms have developed over the past 20 years as online education has taken off - truisms that are now guidelines, indeed requirements, for today's online programs.

- In order for instructors to provide the requisite oversight of students in the distance environment, ideal class size seems to be around 25 students, same as for the traditional career school classroom. This ratio has become embedded in accreditation standards, just like for physical campus operations.

- Because student services are not face to face, career schools have labored to create service practices that are high touch so as to insure student persistence. These include such practices as monitoring attendance and grades via distance. Monitors reach out regularly to students to demonstrate concern and provide counseling for issues students may be experiencing. Since staff is unable to catch online students in the hallways on the way to and from class, very organized and consistent monitoring and outreach programs have proven to be the key to insuring student retention and satisfaction. This gave rise to the hiring of many new staff dedicated solely to servicing the online student population, the cost of which is justified by the value of student retention.

- Multiple studies have shown that a hybrid model of education delivery – one that combines online delivery with campus-based activities such as occasional class meetings and practicum work in the field of study (i.e., labs) – results in better student outcomes such as retention, completion and program satisfaction than in campus-based programs. There are various hybrid models in place throughout the postsecondary industry today.

- Web-enabled distance education opens up a vast world of resources to support student learning and engagement. Perhaps the loss of face to face delivery in the campus model of education is trumped by the explosion of access to unlimited learning resources from around the world. Some say communications among students and between student and instructor is actually enhanced on the online platform.

- Online courses are as, if not more, difficult as the traditionally-delivered course.

- Students are often more eager to transition to online than are instructors.

CURRENT DISTANCE EDUCATION ENROLLMENT – TRADITIONAL AND CAREER SCHOOLS

In fall 2018, there were 6,932,074 students enrolled in any distance education courses at degree-granting postsecondary institutions.

Fully one-third of all college students are enrolled in some form of online course, either fully online or hybrid. This percentage is expected to continue to grow rapidly in response to the worldwide

ENROLLMENT IN DISTANCE EDUCATION PROGRAMS FALL 2018

Number and percentage of students enrolled in degree-granting postsecondary institutions, by distance education participation, and level of enrollment and control of institution: Fall 2018

Level of enrollment and control of institution	Number of students					Percent of students				
			Any distance education course(s)					Any distance education course(s)		
	Total	No distance education courses	Total, any distance education course(s)	At least one, but not all, of student's courses are distance education courses	Exclusively distance education course(s)	Total	No distance education courses	Total, any distance education course(s)	At least one, but not all, of student's courses are distance education courses	Exclusively distance education course(s)
Total	19,645,918	12,713,844	6,932,074	3,674,087	3,257,987	100.0	64.7	35.3	18.7	16.6
Level of enrollment										
Undergraduate	16,610,235	10,885,526	5,724,709	3,399,567	2,325,142	100.0	65.5	34.5	20.5	14.0
PostBaccalaureate	3,035,683	1,828,318	1,207,365	274,520	932,845	100.0	60.2	39.8	9.0	30.7
Control of institution										
Public	14,529,264	9,569,412	4,959,852	3,153,470	1,806,382	100.0	65.9	34.1	21.7	12.4
Private nonprofit	4,134,244	2,878,717	1,255,527	418,048	837,479	100.0	69.6	30.4	10.1	20.3
Private for-profit	982,410	265,715	716,695	102,569	614,126	100.0	27.0	73.0	10.4	62.5

Source: https://nces.ed.gov/programs/digest/d19/ 1

pandemic. It will be interesting to see whether this participation will remain once postsecondary education response returns to normal.

SUMMARY

Sooner or later, it seems you will be asked to teach a course delivered online. Or at the very least, to take a course through distance delivery.

Effective Campus Administrators, Instructional Designers, and Faculty seek to deliver the same quality of courses online as are delivered in their campus classroom. This takes a lot of careful thought in the cycle of planning, design, delivery, and assessment. Over the years, online education has improved through the integration of learning flowing from review of distance course delivery data.

Distance Education is here to stay!